Dedicated to all the co-authors

who have supported me in this task.

Disclaimer

The compiler & editor has tried his level best to edit the write-ups and to provide an error free script. The co-authors have ensured that they have not used any plagiarized content. In case of any plagiarism detected neither the compilers nor the editor holds responsibility. The co-authors are solely responsible for their particular content.

From the Desk of the Editor

A person who writes well and no one knows him/her, it clearly means, (s)he is at an undefined place with their creative heart. Memorable writings that dwell in the ether of human consciousness, cannot be considered as a property of a renowned writer, even these may also be written by a novice.

This is an Anthology of everyone. This Anthology documents many of the great articles, short stories and poems. We did not consider only famous authors, we tried to provide a place for everyone, who is writing well and original. However, it is hard to check that the writing is original or not, that is why, we have prepared a method in which the author has declared that his/her writing, which (s)he is submitting, is originally written by him/her. The talent came out for generation X.

Most often, we need to remain motivated in our tough times. I hope this book will help in encouraging people not only in their tough time but also to move ahead and motivate them to never waste time, even a microsecond. Of course, there are numerous excellent and amazing books available; yet, it is one, which does not equate to less than splendid writings. This Anthology has beauty and essence of creativity, having words & insights of today's era and, written with heart.

Each author is only and full responsible for their own contribution in context of any issue included plagiarism or copyright or any other.

Welcome readers!

Dr. Chandresh Kumar Chhatlani
Editor and Compiler

Contents

Amb. Maid Corbic 9

Anwesha Rath 13

Asila Jaques 16

Asila Jaques 20

Aswin Krishnan 24

Binod Dawadi 28

Dr. R. Shirley Gainneos 34

Jia Monica 39

Michael Otieno Ogelo 42

Muralidhar Bansal 46

Noor Tabassum 48

S. V. Harshini Priyaa 52

Sankalp Mirani 54

Serlina Rose 56

Hafiza Rabia Iqbal 60

Vaneeta Chugh 63

Vimala Thanggavilo 66

Vishal Roy 70

Adriana Rocha......................................72

Deepu Chavan......................................76

Kalpana Bhatt 79

Muralidhar Bansal 82

Ranbir Bhakat 85

Rangeesh Chandrasekar 88

Reshma Samnani 92

Sabita Dakua 96

हिन्दी खंड....................................100

Alkka Jain 101

Ankita Dwivedi..................................107

Archana Kumari 112

Banaso Kumari 117

Jaivir Singh 120

Mrs. Shashi Prakash..............................125

Ms. Pooja Rajesh Nichole 129

Neelaksh 137

Omprakash Kshatriya Prakash 140

Pooja Mishra......................................150

Tejashvi Tripathi 152

Vaishnavi Suthar 155

Vijay Singh Raj 158

आशीष पाण्डेय 161

भावना वधिानी 166

शेख शहज़ाद उस्मानी 170

Anamika 187

Kiran Kumari 195

Mr. Umaji Subhash Patil 199

Nobel Shriwas 204

Rahul Sharma 209

Usha 214

Usha Shrivastava 222

शेख शहज़ाद उस्मानी 227

Vashundhra Yadav 239

डॉ. चंद्रेश कुमार छतलानी / Dr. Chandresh Kumar Chhatlani 241

English

Amb. Maid Corbic

BE JUST WHAT YOU ARE

Always be just what you are, because people know how to be weird in all matters

they know that if you are weak they will attack you when you least find yourself And then as such an act we realize that we are perhaps insignificant beings who will continue to live in an area where each of us can govern each other. and we have to stay motivated if we want to be happy. We are people who have to believe in something supernatural, but also to believe that somewhere far away our happiness is hidden. We must not allow ourselves to be all that we are not, but we must build we have one life that we must give to time, but also to understand that love can overcome everything around us. If possible, we must continue to understand that the motive of life is our destiny which will continue to survive in every echo of life. And how can we continue to believe every day that we believe in ourselves, if we still cannot be all that we are. possible.Motivation mpra to be There is always a key to sincere happiness, but we also believe that somewhere far away we have our luck and the least hope is that we have to defeat some people. What still survives in ourselves is happiness, is the motive when something bad starts us to be strong and optimistic. What is our life today if we do not have a source of sincere happiness and joy in all this and if we must return something better because our destinies are still somewhere in every segment of life, but we must also believe that happiness is far away. What is still alive in ourselves if it is not the choice of a sincere happiness that will describe the world when because all we have is just one notion of life that the motive brings us and motivation is the source of our happiness. We have only one small life that will be described to us, which will be the same color. Love is needed in ourselves if we continue to build the colors of the world, but also that happiness is greater if we give the maximum part of our sincere soul. Motivation is certainly our choice where we will continue to choose all our resources and each of our appearances is just our life is giving something that may be far away there. And love is still described somewhere, happiness is greater when we give maximum to the survival of our trail, and finally our lesson for life is to continue to build a sense of happiness that we must not easily forget . Therefore, faith and hope is only for our world to continue to be shortened, for motivation to lie somewhere in everything. Therefore, be what you are and do not allow yourself to continue to be what you are not, because all this with which we must not turn lightly. The lesson of everything is that life is wonderful if we have someone with us and that we must not forget that people were created to motivate each other. The lesson is that people are born to be what they are. The meaning of life is the motivation that must lie within ourselves. And everything will be over and over.

-0-

Author's Profile

Maid Corbic from Tuzla, 22 years old. In his spare time he writes poetry that repeatedly praised as well as rewarded. He also selflessly helps others around him, and he is moderator of the World Literature Forum WLFPH (World Literature Forum Peace and Humanity) for humanity and peace in the world in Bhutan. He is also the editor of the First Virtual Art portal led by Dijana Uherek Stevanovic. Many works have also been published in anthologies and journals (Chile, Spain, Ecuador, Bosnia and Herzegovina, San Salvador, United Kingdom, Indonesia).

detrix233@gmail.com

+38761870875

Declaration by Author:

This is my original content. I have copyright for this write-up & I am providing project head to use it for publishing with my name.

- Amb. Maid Corbic, Bosnia and Herzegovina

Anwesha Rath

Girls today

Break your silence

Raise voice against violence

Stop seeing wrong

But stand strong

Be own

Becoming dependent

Fight for your independence

Make your future bright

Make the dreams light

Change the society eye sight

Let's other stop

But remember for own

You gave to fight

Yourself, you will define

Become a inspiration

Let's do motivation

Start a new creation

Create a new nation

Now begin your journey.

-O-

Author's Profile

Anwesha Rath, A girl from small town used to see huge dreams now is working in anthologies is just 19 years old doing graduation her aim is just to take care of her parents as they cared for her till her dream is not writing poems but to share heartfelt message..

anwesha988@gmail.com

08252026998

Declaration by Author:

This is my original content. I have copyright for this write-up & I am providing project head to use it for publishing with my name.

Anwesha Rath, India

Asila Jaques

WOMEN : GOD'S PRECIOUS GIFT

She is like water,

And is a faithful daughter.

Life is impossible without her,

She's always with you forever.

She is a candle,

 And a wonderful example.

Her life is full of inspiration,

Because of her hardwork and dedication.

She is a dreamer, a achiever.

 Been always taught to be a winner.

She has the heart to care,

And a mind just to be there.

She has the soul of storm,

And freedom of wind.

Eyes like a shining star,

with moonshine within.

She is the sea,

with a successful key.

She's the daughter of earth,

Since her success of birth.

She is the lightning on toes,

And changes the world where-ever she goes.

 she's the fire and wood,

And land and water that makes the earth.

SHE IS A' WOMEN'

- Asila Jaques

-0-

Author's Profile

Asila Jaques D/o Francisco X. Jaques and
Sinforosa L. Rebelo, from Goa - India, born
on 5th December 2006 is a co - author, and a
multi talented all-rounder child and have
achieved many awards and prizes at state,
national and international level in the field of
drawing /painting, poetry writing, essay
writing, hand writing/creative writing,
greeting card making /design, poster making
photography, creative arts etc. She have
achieved more than 500+ certificates of
appreciations, achievement, merit, pledge,
completion, Self IQ,quiz and participation,
from National and international
organizations too. She is 1 time selected and
2 times awarded the International diamond
artist award and is 2 times noble book of
world record holder. Appreciated by Indian
star book of records. she is officially

appointed as a international peace
ambassador in the year 2020 and
International Peace Matrix 2020 winner in
poster making. she achieved many awards at
state, national and international level.

asilajaques@gmail.com

7038394379

<u>Declaration by Author:</u>

This is my original content. I have copyright
for this write-up & I am providing project
head to use it for publishing with my name.

Asila Jaques, India

Asila Jaques

ALWAYS THERE FOR ME.

You've been there in the terrors of night;

Till my sun and the day glow up bright .

You made me perfect When I was not ;

You gave me hand when I was lost.

You taught me to be brave ;

In your big arms I'm always safe.

No one can replace your place ;

You are my Dad by God's grace .

You're so loving and kind,

A father with a generous mind .

Always taught me to be strong ;

Didn't let anything go wrong .

You always found out the best in me;

You saw the talent that world couldn't see.

You walked my side in good and bad ;

You are a 'True real man Dad'.

You are so gentle and strong ;

In all situations, correct or wrong.

Your love is so rich and pure;

It's a medicine for all pain, its a cure.

Your love plays a very big part;

In my life and in my heart.

A big thank you for listening and caring;

And for giving and sharing.

   -Asila Jaques

-0-

<u>Author's Profile</u>

Asila Jaques D/o Francisco X. Jaques and Sinforosa L. Rebelo, from Goa - India, born on 5th December 2006 is a co - author, and a multi talented all-rounder child and have achieved many awards and prizes at state, national and international level in the field of drawing /painting, poetry writing, essay writing, hand writing/creative writing, greeting card making /design, poster making photography, creative arts etc. She have achieved more than 500+ certificates of appreciations, achievement, merit, pledge, completion, Self IQ,quiz and participation, from National and international organizations too. She is 1 time selected and 2 times awarded the International diamond artist award and is 2 times noble book of world record holder. Appreciated by star book of records. she is officially appointed as a international peace ambassador in the year 2020 and International Peace Matrix 2020 winner in poster making. she achieved many awards at state, national and international level.

asilajaques@gmail.com

7038394379

<u>Declaration by Author:</u>

This is my original content. I have copyright for this write-up & I am providing project head to use it for publishing with my name.

-Asila Jaques

Aswin Krishnan

Toxicity and Motivation

The state at which a humans personality and mental state can be .p as Toxicity... This Toxicity gets into us through demotivation, belittling, advices, challenges, directions/instructions humiliation and mockery. Everyone in this world are surrounded by situations and people in which comprises of any of such instances.

We tolerate such people & situation for keeping our family's prestige and loyalty of our friends and acquaintances and we keep the pain of our injured minds undisclosed subtle so that it doesn't cause any impact on the circles we belong to.

But as we continue to stay quiet, the circumstances worsen and we are forced to encounter with people, occurrences, and instances where such a person is always rejected and harassed at least by verbal means which always makes a harsh impact on our mental health and stability

Such impacts leads to serious mental trauma like dejections, depression introvercy and unnecessary inferiority thoughts which in turn turns into criminal minds or sell destructive thoughts which is both socially and individually harmful

So, next time when you see someone facing such a toxic situation, instead of joining with others try and help them overcome it. Take them to their passion let them make a signature in this world, Talk to them about the improvisation they can make, express your feedback generously energize them to stay engaged, try to generate the pleasure of fulfillment in them, accept them and appreciate them.

Make them feel worthy of themselves, try educating the others about the victim's mental trauma and state of worthlessness they may suffer. Provide the victims with necessary emotional support and belongingness. Also help them to get medical support if necessary. Because Everyone in this world is beautiful and unique in their own ways.

<u>Author's Profile</u>

ASWIN KRISHNAN resides at Ottapalam Palakkad which in South India situated in Kerala.He is studying in B.com 1st year and focused to get Government job. His hobbies are watching Movies, Writing, Playing Keyboard and Music hearing in free time. For more details of his creative writings you can visit instagram account as below-

ASWIN KRISHNAN resides at Ottapalam Palakkad which in South India situated in Kerala.He is studying in B.com 1st year and focused to get Government job. His hobbies are watching Movies, Writing, Playing Keyboard and Music hearing in free time. For more details of his creative writings you can visit instagram account mentioned as below

@fosthoughts

aswinkrishnancotp@gmail.com

8606612593

<u>**Declaration by Author:**</u>

This is my original content. I have copyright for this write-up & I am providing project head to use it for publishing with my name.

ASWIN KRISHNAN, India

Binod Dawadi

The Love And Wish For All The Women And Mother's Of The World

The Love and Wish For All The Women and Mothers Of The World

Mother you are a girl. You are facing the life of the girl at your childhood. You are facing the life of the woman after your marriage. You are facing the difficulties and obstacles in your life. You are rearing and caring . You need to satisfy your husband. You need to satisfy your children. You need to give satisfaction to your family. You are the form of the God.

Mother you also gave birth to me. Not only me mother's you gave birth to the whole world. You have the power and strength of making children. Rearing them. Making them aware about their life. Teaching them always good moral lessons in a life to be a good man. Mother you are never doing other or indifference to your children.

When children are doing some mistakes. You are hiding that mistakes and taking that mistakes in your hand. You have the capability of taking the risks. You can handle any difficult situation in your life. You can win this world. You can do each and every things in your life. You can give birth which is the most difficult work in this world. You can rear and care children until for your last breathe.

You care and love children more than anyone in this world. Only women can know the pains of the women. Women you are God teaching the children good and bad. Making their aware of their problems and difficulties in their life. Your sacrifices and values could not be explained by these words.

Your blood gives life to the baby. Your breathe gives life to the baby. Your body's organs are helping you to work in excellence for the baby. After nine months of pregnancy your body composes and creates the shape of the body from the waters. It is the most magical thing. Then only you give birth. You are the greatest than anyone in this world.

You are always wanting the bright future of your child. I am also one of the son of the mother her name is Ambika Dawadi. I want to give billions thanks for my mother and thanks for the mothers of world.

Who gave birth to a good son like me who will always praise and love about a women and mothers of the world. By realizing their contribution and their sacrifices towards our life. Mother I can't give you anything.

I have not any big contributions like yours like you gave in my life. Thank you for God for making women, father man and the mother. So we forgot the women and we always dominate and discriminate women's in most part of the world. So we should love and care them. This is small love and wish for all the women and mothers of the world. They may have got difficulties and obstacles may God always brings happiness and success in their life. Their love and dedication may also continues to the future and will be immortal for the time when this Universe will exist.

Mother be happy and be good give birth,
rare them and make their future bright.
Mothers you are welcome in this world and
we all the children of this world want your
sympathy and love. You are greater than any
thing. Nothing can be compared as well as
kept in your place. Your essence is so much
in a life. There are many kinds of the
happiness from your support in our life. You
will be immortal in our life. We give our all
thanks to all the women, girls, fathers men
as well as mothers of this world.

Summary

This article is trying to show us the
importance of the mother, girl, or women.
Their life their struggles and their obstacles.
The life of their towards difficulties and
obstacles. Towards their vision and thoughts
for their children. Their love, care, support
for the family. To memorize their works.
Their dedication their values and importance
in our life. They are giving life to children. By
losing their life sometimes at the birth also.
Their works for the better future of the
children as well as families.

But men are thinking about women they are the informal. They don't go to the offices. They don't do the house works properly. But in reality the women are doing more things then the men. To give birth to a baby. To love and care them. To make them able. This is the greatest thing that a women can do in their life. Sometimes from these works women are feeling that they are inside the four corners of the houses. Always sitting and working there. But men should always remember and realise the problems as well as difficulties of the life of the women. We should love and care them. As they do to their children as for their families and societies.

©® Binod Dawadi

Nepal

-0-

Author's Profile

He is Binod Dawadi from Purano Naikap 13, Kathmandu, Nepal. He has completed his Master's Degree in Major English. His hobbies are reading, writing, watching movies, traveling etc. He is a writer, teacher and a social worker. He has created many articles, poems and stories. He is a very sociable person. He doesn't wastes his time by doing nothing. He is always engaged in some critical things. He is always helping to the poor people in the society. He likes to spend his time with friends with talking and traveling. He is a kind and gentle boy.

vinoddawadi9@gmail.com

9.7798605135e+12

<u>Declaration by Author:</u>

This is my original content. I have copyright for this write-up & I am providing project head to use it for publishing with my name.

Binod Dawadi, Nepal

Dr. R. Shirley Gainneos

MOTIVATION

"You are the artist of your own life. Don't hand the paintbrush to anyone else".

We are in control of our lives. Each and every one of us have a different role to follow. Sometimes, we tend to forget our role, and decide to be like somebody else. It is good to keep someone as a role model, but changing ourselves in order to completely become like someone else is dangerous. Give yourself permission to be great. Choose yourself right now. Don't wait for someone else to do it.

We often forget the positive aspects of our lives and look deeper into the negative aspects.

If you are positive about things, you are hopeful and confident, and think of the good aspects of a situation rather than the bad ones. We should appreciate ourselves for all the small successes we've achieved. If we come across failures, we must remember to use it as a motivation to push ourselves forward. Failures are there to mold us. So we shouldn't get disheartened by failures. Feel happy for whatever you achieve no matter how it is big. Just celebrate your little achievement . Don't think how many people join you in your small success. Just enjoy for yourself. Be happy.

Sometimes, we let other people to take control of our lives. We let other people to set the rules for us. Everyone is gifted with an inbuilt quality or an inherent talent that is unique to that individual. Our life is our responsibility. So we must give it all we've got.

Never give up in life. The problems which we face in life are just like obstacles. We must overcome those obstacles with courage. Then we will be able to achieve success. Never let the obstacles to block your goal.

Always aim high. Aim for the moon; but if you miss, you'll land on a star. If you miss the goal, you'll still have achieved something. It indicates that even if things don't go as planned, they still can turn out to be a success. If you're aiming for something, even if you don't achieve it, you'll still be somewhere better than where you started.

Never compare our lives with others. Each and everyone is unique and we have a different role to play. Don't compare your chapter 1 with someone else's chapter 15. You can control one life – yours. When we consistently compare ourselves to others, we waste precious energy focusing on other peoples' lives rather than our own. Comparing yourself to others will always cause you to regret what you aren't, rather than allow you to enjoy life as who you are. It will always steal the joy and happiness that is within your reach... and place it just outside of your reach instead.

If you want to be happy and get success, paint your wish with your brush. Most of the time we face illogical sadness like if some one criticize, you then you totally get upset, but there is no point in getting upset. It depends on you how you want to get this criticize for yourself. Don't stop at that criticize point. Just move on and think what you like most. It is difficult, but when you learn to deal this technique you will feel relaxed and happy. Don't loose your temper because there is no use of your temper. It only depends on what you want to become and how to get. Move on with your desire. We should live our life according to our principles, and not be governed by the opinion of others.

We are the artist of our life. We are the masters. Don't just make life work; make it a masterpiece. It is we who decided our fate. Life is short. Don't take one day for granted. Everything can change in a moment. Be grateful for all you have and all that you are.

"Do you want to know who you are? Don't ask. Act! Action will delineate and define you." —Thomas Jefferson

-0-

Author's Profile

Dr. Shirley is a dentist from Nagercoil. She is fond of writing a lot of stories and poems. She has been writing ever since she was young. She likes to read a lot of books written by different authors and poets. Her other interests include painting, sketching, travelling, photography, singing, listening to music and playing the piano.

dr.shirleygainneos.r@gmail.com

9003543388

Declaration by Author:

This is my original content. I have copyright for this write-up & I am providing project head to use it for publishing with my name.

Dr. R. Shirley Gainneos, India

Jia Monica

Truth be Told, Introvert

"I'm not crazy, my reality is just different than yours."

- Chesire Cat

Introverts are a very interesting group of people. We are often misunderstood. Yes, I am an introvert too. Social interactions drain my energy. And most of the times my intuition and feelings get the best of me. I sometimes feel like I have to carry the weight of the world. Because unlike what most people think, being an introvert does not mean that you don't care about others. Oftentimes, it's quiet the contrary. You care too much about others. But it is the fear of beong rejected that makes you awkward in social situations. You want to help others, but you feel like you don't fit in so you just spend time alone in your own world. You have the strongest desire in making the world a better place.

And truth be told, introvert, you can. You are not alone. People like me and you can still make a difference in our own little ways. Sure, it is not easy. We don't have to come out of our comfort zone because unlike other people, some of us performs our best working by ourselves. And that's okay. Some people may not get it but you just have to stop thinking about their opinions. Think of ways how to take care of yourself, how to love yourself. Because how can we give something that we don't have in ourselves?

Stop overthinking, or limit it. For your mind is so fragile, if you don't take care of it, who will?

They said we are the quiet ones. That's okay. We are not talkers, we are doers. Truth be told, introvert, you are.

-0-

Author's Profile

Jia Monica is a poetess, ghostwriter of romance novels and up and coming author of her novels plus co-author of a few poetry anthology. She balances her full-time corporate work, family, writing and becoming a business owner with the help of self-love, confidence, time management and few cups of coffee. It is her desire to help others do it, too... Minus the few cups of coffee for those who prefers tea.

jia.castro.micah@gmail.com

6.3955907328e+11

Declaration by Author:

This is my original content. I have copyright for this write-up & I am providing project head to use it for publishing with my name.

Jia Monica, Philippines

Michael Otieno Ogelo

ENCOURAGING BOOK READING

As the world continues to grow, the technology also develops. People can easily use the digital devices with ease in communication, conducting some businesses especially the online business, getting some entertainment, developing videos, music... and many others.

As most people are clouded with technology, some are resistance to technology especially those with less knowledge in the technology. This at times brings challenge to the book readers particularly those who are deeply rooted in the use of technology as their day to day business.

Reading culture is poor in some nations like the developing countries which is seen to be striving with their livelihood in order to bring the food on the table. So, less or no time is created for book reading.

Young children and the grown ups are often seen to love watching videos, movies, playing video games... among others hence leaving no time for book reading. This culture is trending and it brings a challenge to the book industry.

Reading books is good. See, you develop your vocabulary, your reading skills also get improved, your cognitive strength also improves, you also get skills to apply on negotiation table, you also get story to tell your friends or family members... among others.

So, let's minimize the use of technological devices at the expense of forgetting our books. Books are good and let's encourage everyone to go back to the books and dig much knowledge for educational, entertainment and debatable purposes. This will change the face of our society in terms of morality.

-0-

Author's Profile

Michael Otieno Ogelo is an author born in Nyakach Sub-county, Kisumu county, Kenya Republic. He holds Diploma in Special Needs and Inclusive Education from Maseno University, Kenya.

He began writing in 2018, and in 2021, he published his first book called "Peer Coalition and Other Stories." The book comprises of five interesting and humorous stories which emanates from the modern world society like: corruption, covid-19 documentary, terrorism act... among others.

Michael has also participated in various joint writing of different anthologies as A Co-Author, hence winning many certificates of publication, letters of appreciation and e-trophies. He believes in hard work.

Contacts: Twitter: @ogelomichael

Email: mikeogelo@gmail.com

mikeogelo@gmail.com

+254701266459

Muralidhar Bansal

Woman- A warrior post marriage

A woman gets a new life after marriage. Some work as housewives whereas some as helping hands. She has the such will power that can crush any obstacles coming her family's way. She equally manages time for both house and work. She fulfils her responsibilities as a daughter (in-law) at home and her duties as a leader in work. She fulfils all her promises made to the members in the family. Its her charisma that never lets her enthusiasm go down in vain.

A woman, after marriage balances her family and work. She earns for her family and feeds it. What actually she is? This answer is only with her. The burden of starving family, scorching sun and the workload of office; these all can be handled by a super natural power i.e. a woman who is a daughter, a mother, a sister and many more avatars she has.

-0-

Author's Profile

HE IS MURALIDHAR BANSAL FROM NEPAL HE
LOVES WRITING AND STARTED WRITING
WHEN HE WAS A STUDENT. PLAYING
CRICKET AND WRITING ARE HIS HOBBIES.

muralidhar_agrawal55@yahoo.co.in

009779812360238

Declaration by Author:

This is my original content. I have copyright
for this write-up & I am providing project
head to use it for publishing with my name.

Muralidhar Bansal, Nepal

Noor Tabassum

IS THERE A REASON FOR LIFE?

Life is an unpredictable journey from birth to death. What holds for us the next moment is unknown. It is a beautiful journey that we undergo with many people surrounding us. Every living thing has its significance in this realm. The Almighty is creating everything was a reason. Mountains are created for acting as pegs to hold this earth; water bodies are created so that they undergo a water cycle that continues to supply water to living things unstoppably.

Similarly, every living thing has its significance. Plants and trees supply oxygen and food. When everything has so much importance, do you think our creation has no reason? We are created for a very significant reason. We are given high intelligence, which excels every creature.

It is such a blessing to be born as human beings. We are sent down to earth so that we can enjoy every minute beauty of this world. We are sent down so that we love and spread peace and tranquillity. We were sent down to be rulers who rule this earth with justice and harmony. Our intelligence was given to make this earth worth living. We were sent to tolerate each other and to spread the smile. That is why Our Master sent us here for a limited period.

But are we truly doing what we were sent for? Are we spreading love, peace, and smiles? In the quest to prove we are the best, we are destroying this world and making it hell. We are happily spreading pollution, killing other living creatures, and destroying their homes. We are using our intelligence for the wrong purpose as our eyes are covered with dark glasses of greed, hatred, and jealousy.

Let us remember the purpose of our existence and lead meaningful and happy life.

-0-

Author's Profile

The name of the author is Noor Tabassum. Writing is her passion. She has participated in more than 300 anthologies as co author and has also written solo books called Sensibles, Twisted Firsts and Adorable Prod. She is a nature lover and loves to lead a simple life. She expresses all her feelings in her writings as she thinks it is the most powerful medium to communicate. She has won many writing competitions, and her articles have been published in many magazines too. She enjoys writing poems and short stories. Her stories have been published in the Times of India newspaper too. Her Instagram id is @noortabassumali123.

noortabassumali123@gmail.com

+971504636123

<u>**Declaration by Author:**</u>

This is my original content. I have copyright for this write-up & I am providing project head to use it for publishing with my name.

Noor Tabassum, United Arab Emirates

S. V. Harshini Priyaa

Success Awaits

There's a common saying that,

"Defeat the defeat, before the defeat defeats you."

Do not be afraid of defeat, keep trying. You could win over today or tommorow. Never think defeat as a failure. Even don't be dejected of failure. A wise person knows that the first step of success is defeat.

Let's take a case study of Thomas Edison :

"I have not failed. I've just found ten thousand ways that won't work."

Here, you can feel the positivity in his mind that he has changed a defeat (negative thing for common people) into positive.

Our life is somewhat like that. We may face many defeats or sorrows while doing something. We have to achieve our goal in a positive way by Defeating the defeat.

Only take your failures as a wrong path to your goal, and start a new and a positive way way to journey.... Now success awaits for you.

-0-

Author's Profile

Harshini Priyaa is a talented girl in drawing, singing and event managing. She is a blogger, poetess, youtuber, compiler and an artist. She is a co-author of 50+ anthologies. She has written the novel "The Land Of Horrible Nightmares", online and it has crossed many views.

harshipriyaa@gmail.com

7338957385

Declaration by Author:

This is my original content. I have copyright for this write-up & I am providing project head to use it for publishing with my name.

S. V. Harshini Priyaa, India

Sankalp Mirani

Devil

You are the one I admire

You are the one who love to inspire

As cold blooded as ice and as hot as fire

Don't try this with your siblings bloody liar

You are great even if you were casted to Hades

By your own father's spades you were saved by your mom and Mazikeen's tongue

Love you till the end

Love you till the hell

Even if after this father rings the bell and takes me to the death knell.

-O-

Author's Profile

Sankalp is petricia pierra of his life, he is fooled by someone and all the great people in the world, he will reach heights, he will make it big . We will kill them all in quest of peace.

sankalpmirani610@gmail.com

08830213375

<u>Declaration by Author:</u>

This is my original content. I have copyright for this write-up & I am providing project head to use it for publishing with my name.

Sankalp Mirani, India

Serlina Rose

Motivational Poetry

1. Senryu 1

Backward never but,

To heal, resolve and release

Hate to transform life!

2. Love is forgiveness (Tanka)

Imprisoned with hate, our

Minds commit treasons

But to be happy with love

Find strength and comfort

In forgiveness to wrongs mourn!

3. Senryu 2

With delicate words

Hard heart soften with standards

Open up meekly.

4. Gratitude (Tanka)

A display of gratitude

Goes a long way to

Someone with a doleful heart,

And an ungrateful

Person is bane to glad hearts!

5. Don't Give Up (Limerick)

Despite the struggles, whatever the pain,

You can achieve all, find courage again.

Work hard, don't settle, confirm.

Ambition's mindset that's firm.

Accomplishments display quitting is vain.

6. Senryu 3

Loyal trust –

Like feeble hands of the aged

Once crumbled can't be replaced!

☐☐2022©SerlinaRose☐☐✍☐

<u>**Author's Profile**</u>

Serlina Rose is a Dominican poetess & writer, born & raised on the Caribbean island of Dominica. Serlina's writing aspirations are to publish her poetry collection (Serlina's Poesy Anthology) & Later, her first romance novel. Blessed with the scenery & environment of nature, Serlina has used the gift of writing to compile pieces that showcase her scenery, home island & to express her views; and with a love for writing & composing, has submitted a few poems for publications which has appeared in these Anthologies: Poetrypea journal of haiku & senryu: Autumn edition 2020; The Dancing Light of Dawn: #InstantEternal poetry vol. 1, 2021; An Anthology for a friend by Victoria Hartman 2021; Unhealed Secrets by Jessica Sandra Toppa 2022; My Tale of Life by Nisha Nigam 2022; Women & Empowerment by Sahiba Irshad Wani, 2022; Unspoken Words by Spotwrite Publications (Bhawna Surana);

767SerlinaRose@gmail.com

+17672953559

Hafiza Rabia Iqbal

"Motivation"

"The synonym of hope is motivation."

Motivation gives us strength and courage to face the bitter realities in a positive way, it doesn't matter if you are motivated no problems come in your way, the thing is that you are able to handle them in a good way manners instead of letting down your and blaming others. For me if you can inject someone motivation you are doing something great and in life when you're needed it badly it will come in double amount so, do the good thing without demanding something in return, because reward can only give you Allah and Allah like the person who is more beneficial for His creation in any way and saying something good to anyone is Sadqa e Jaria.

God bless all of us! Aamin sum a aamin

Syedah

-0-

Author's Profile

Syedah Hafiza Rabia Iqbal, belongs to Pakistan. She's an artist, published writer, co-author, compiler and calligrapher as well, she has been participated in national and international writing contests. She has been completed her master in English and Urdu literature and linguistics as well. She's an animal lover and having deep affiliation with nature. She wants to spread peace and positivity and purpose of her writing is to reveal realities and highlights the social issues. Her favorite genre is poetry. She's a motivational speaker and by profession an English teacher.

@syedah91

shrabiaiqbal@gmail.com

shrabiaiqbal@gmail.com

03098126629

Vaneeta Chugh

Yes I can, I can do!

Does it feel strange to hear these words from someone else's mouth on a regular basis like a mantra of lord is being chanted non-stop?

Are you one of those people who don't believe in affirmations or creating their own life?

Have you given up your life solely in the hands of your destiny?

If that had been the case with you till now, I would urge you to stop living in the illusion and start living your life to the fullest!

Do you call it living, where you don't have the power to choose in your own hands?

This is worse thah death!

If you have been dying each passing second under the cumbersome weight of lamentation and fate, you are no more than a bloody carcass!

Your hands aren't just hands, but the magic tool to craft your life, with your mind being the powerful weapon to put your dreams to reality!

You must have heard the quote, "if you believe you can, you really can!

And note down,

You have the power to choose your beliefs!

Your beliefs are only your choice!

So, if you wanna reach the pinnacle of success, start believing and reciting,

"Yes I can, I can do!"

-0-

Author's Profile

Vaneeta Chugh, a graduate in b.com and diplomad in special education (visual impairment), born and brought up in Delhi. She is soaring beyond the pinnacle of her dreams. She loves penning down soulful wonders and reviving a new cosmos through her quill. Her passion is to be the legendary Wordsmith.

vaneetachugh06@gmail.com

+918377050374

Declaration by Author:

This is my original content. I have copyright for this write-up & I am providing project head to use it for publishing with my name.

Vaneeta Chugh, India

Vimala Thanggavilo
Refine and Define

Mentality and attitude need seriousness. It's to all kinds of issues that occur or are raised at current moments.

Let's together take a step forward. Empathy in real life.

Allow the individual to measure impact or influence by others towards major current issues.

Take charge of changes before expecting and provoking issues.

It's a method to bring back the prosperous within to reflect.

Flourishing oneself is most important. Ever since each was enacted, issues would be suppressed or resolved generously.

Nothing can grow without oneness permission. All guidelines and knowledge preached or shared by Speakers, Motivators, Religious, Spiritual Masters, Teachers, News

Creators, and many others are for us to
extract the essence and bloom on our own.

On another side of life, struggles are not your
fault, as they may seem calm without
knowing the depth of it. No one can detect
or predict as they find it too difficult why it's
happening, even if they are leading a positive
life. One must remember that everything is a
consequence of doing good or bad. It also
doesn't always turn out as we expect. Due to
unknown reasons, we just need to trust
humans born with all attributes and every
drop of life challenges is common to
everyone.

Simple but not easy as one just need to pass
through it and keep in mind that every time
one falls from a certain height, nature's law
will ensure you are safely landing on the
ground. As life needs to go on with all the
flaws as it has been designed for us.

The same mistakes are not wise to repeat.
Keep moving forward!

Accumulate the knowledge and experiences
to step out forward to another phase of life

whereby self-awareness of all the advantages and disadvantages will be added on.

Always feel in tune with the universe and engage with mind, soul, and body as it leads this journey.

Be Dare! Be Aware! Be Alert!

-0-

Author's Profile

Ms. Vimala is the youngest daughter of Mr. & Mrs. S.Thanggavilo M.Thevanai. She was born and living in Malaysia. Written more than 200 quotes and poems. All were published via Instagram page @fun_luv_joy and @uninterruptible_quotes. Launched as Co-Author for a few books. We on her behalf are grateful to her family, compiler, publisher, followers, readers, and supporters for this great opportunity and support. Thank you.

lald_tv@yahoo.com

60123220775

<u>**Declaration by Author:**</u>

This is my original content. I have copyright for this write-up & I am providing project head to use it for publishing with my name.

Vimala Thanggavilo, Malaysia

Vishal Roy

Mountains

The mountains told me a story .

that if you want to live then be like me.

Live with self-respect, be firm to your goal,
whatever the situation,

be it like a storm, a thunderstorm or rain
whatever you face with courage.

 Never make yourself feel helpless

-0-

<u>Author's Profile</u>

This is Vishal Kumar Roy (Vishu) and he
belongs from

Dhanbad (Jharkhand). He/she is currently
working in

private sector. He likes to write.

Vishalroy241@gmail.com

8789349311

Adriana Rocha
You

Look at me well,

look at my eyes

and my fleshy lips,

look at my black hair

dancing in the wind,

listen to me carefully,

my sensual voice pronounces

phrases that make

many people tremble,

but deep down

they are important truths

which narrate facts

that echo.

Feel the fire in my hugs,

warm enough

to provide shelter.

The beat of my heart

is accelerated by

those whom I love,

watch me transform into

a beast that fights

for what is fair and true.

You are in front of a person,

a human being

that feels and understands

this is a strange world,

but in spite of everything,

look at me,

shining and dancing

on the edge of the tragedy,

when I play with fire,

I am often burned,

but I love to blaze.

Look at me

being the protagonist

of my own story,

watch me walk

in the fire of calamities,

look at me rise

from the ashes,

transforming

the collapsed rubble

into the new walls

of my strength.

-0-

Author's Profile

Adriana Rocha was born in Bolivia. She is a
psychologist who teaches English to business
administration, odontology, medicine and
law students. Poetry, photography and

educational psychology are her passions. Her journey into the world of words has started in 2019. She has been participating in different literary events in Latin America, Spain and India.

yuthielful@gmail.com

+1 (862) 264-3876

<u>Declaration by Author:</u>

This is my original content. I have copyright for this write-up & I am providing project head to use it for publishing with my name.

Adriana Rocha, Bolivia

Deepu Chavan

Inspirational program

Once their was a student who always use to do some art work, drawing, painting, sports. But in studies he was always less interested. This was a very disappointed to their parents. They use to say him daily to read well and score more marks. But the boy was not taking it seriously. One find day their was a program in his college about great personalities. Boy was not interested about the program he thought it was boring. But, his friends took him to the program. He sat listening to all great personalities and was imagining he was on the spot. And he thought he should also become just different than others. On the fine day due to speech his mind changed. He took the inspiration and motivation by all great figures. After few years he was a great business person.

-0-

Author's Profile

This is Deepu Chavan from Bengaluru, Karnataka. Born on 22nd July 2001 in a tiny little village called Nagpuri (Arisikere), Hassan, Karnataka. Spent school life in Vijaya Bharathi school (T-Dasarahalli), Bengaluru from pre-nursery to 3rd standard and from 4th to 10th in Blossom school (Bagalagunta), Bengaluru. 11th and 12th in BGS PU College (Hessarghatta), Bengaluru. Presently doing Bachelor's in B.sc Genetics (2nd Year) in Padmashree Institute of Management and Science (Kengri), Bengaluru. Hobbies are Reading books, writing books, art work, Singing, dancing, Badminton, Tennis and Reading different subjects to gain knowledge.

chavanmanoj2001@gmail.com / 8310502561

Declaration by Author:

This is my original content. I have copyright for this write-up & I am providing project head to use it for publishing with my name.

Deepu Chavan, India

Kalpana Bhatt

The Unsaid

After many years when Aruna returned to her hometown she was wondering about what would have happened to her childhood friends. As she could recollect a few of them, actually she was returning home from mental asylum after many years..As the taxi was arriving her House.. she could recollect many a things

She made the taxi to stop near a tree ...

Yes! This was the tree, the very tree... And she was banged into her past

"Hey, Aruna ... Leave me...I have to go...My parents have arranged my marriage, and I have to listen to them..As the girl's father is paying us 50 lacs as dowry...." He was laughing...

Aruna had known him since her school days and when they reached youth..They were in love. Days and months and years of

togetherness... And what was he saying...
Means her love was selling himself...But
why..

He continued, "listen Aruna, I have 2 younger
sisters you know them right!

Elder one Rakhi is getting married to an
industrialist... And they are asking for 30
lacs...

And the younger one as you know is in last
year of engineering .

Father is a retired person...My job is not
sufficient for my family...

Aruna was just staring at her love... His
words were pouring stones on her heart and
emotions...

Within no times he was gone...

She had caught hold of his hand, but...

Suddenly some one called her there which
had made her come out from her memories

It was Him, her love Rakesh...

He wanted to say something...

But Aruna ...

-0-

Author's Profile

A learner who wishes to know and
understand literature.

klpna_bhatt@yahoo.com

9424473377

Declaration by Author:

This is my original content. I have copyright
for this write-up & I am providing project
head to use it for publishing with my name.

Kalpana Bhatt, India

Muralidhar Bansal

ONE THING THAT I WANTED TO TELL MY PARENTS

Parents are the paradise in the earth itself. God couldn't reach everyehere. So they sent parents to the earth. One thing I always wanted to tell my parents and that is about my interest and hobby.

My parents had a dream to see me as a C.A. but i would tell them my interest in business.

May be a CA is paid more, but a business is a business be it from small knot bolt to a big iron industry. Wealth is at the both ways, but in business there is aspiration with inspiration. I would convince them that i would earn more with more hard work but whatever i would be earning; it would be under their surveillance.

As a CA, I might remain a book worm, but in business i would have more scopes, more behaviour, more relationship and there would be parent's guidance too

I would tell them not to worry for me
because anything that happens; happens for
good and if i am honest and sincere in my
dreams, I know my parents would be happier
than any other degrees in life.

Thus, i would tell them that business is in my
blood and if i design my business in a better
way, I would get the best shape of a leader in
near future.

-0-

<u>Author's Profile</u>

HE IS MURALIDHAR BANSAL FROM NEPAL HE
LOVES WRITING AND STARTED WRITING
WHEN HE WAS A STUDENT. PLAYING
CRICKET AND WRITING ARE HIS HOBBIES.

muralidhar_agrawal55@yahoo.co.in

009779812360238

Ranbir Bhakat

THE ELEPHANT ROPE

As a man was passing the elephants, he suddenly stopped, confused by the fact that these huge creatures were being held by only a small rope tied to their front leg. No chains, no cages. It was obvious that the elephants could, at anytime, break away from their bonds but for some reason, they did not.

He saw a trainer nearby and asked why these animals just stood there and made no attempt to get away. "Well," trainer said, "when they are very young and much smaller we use the same size rope to tie them and, at that age, it's enough to hold them. As they grow up, they are conditioned to believe they cannot break away. They believe the rope can still hold them, so they never try to break free."

The man was amazed. These animals could at any time break free from their bonds but because they believed they couldn't, they were stuck right where they were.

Failure is part of learning; we should never give up the struggle in life.

-0-

Author's Profile

Author by heart and passion.

Writing since He was 16.

His writeups touches reality and reaches everyone's heart. After publishing his own book he wants to explore more. He wants to grasp and grow in his writing journey.

Wrote about 250+ Anthologies & 2 Solo Book in preparation.

Gmail: ranbirbhakat5456@gmail.com

Insta Id: @_writing__tales_

ranbirbhakat5456@gmail.com

7586026247

<u>**Declaration by Author:**</u>

This is my original content. I have copyright for this write-up & I am providing project head to use it for publishing with my name.

Ranbir Bhakat, India

Rangeesh Chandrasekar

How can we give a Human Being a zero ?

A student studying in Russia says:

The highest score for most of the exams in Russia is 5.

If a student does not answer any question and returns back his exam paper blank, with no question answered, he gets 2 out of 5.

In my first days at the University of Moscow, I did not know about this system and I was surprised and asked Dr. Theodor Medraev: "Is this fair that a student did not answer any question and you give him 2 out of 5? Why not give him a zero ?

Isn't that the right way ?"

He answered:

"How can we give a Human Being a zero ?

How can we give him a zero to someone who was getting up at 7 am to attend all the lectures ?

How can we give him a zero since he got up in this cold weather, and used public transport and reached to do the exam in time, and tried to solve the questions ?

How can we give him a zero for the nights he used to study and spent his money on pens and notebooks and bought a computer for studying ?

How can we give him a zero when he left all other life styles and pursued his studies ?

Here my son, we do not give a zero to a student just because he did not know the answer.

We at least try to respect the fact that this is a Human Being, and he is having a brain, and he tried. Because this result which we give, is not just for the questions in the exam paper, it is also about showing appreciation and respect to the fact that this is a Human Being and deserves to have a score."

Truly I cried and did not know how to respond.

There I knew my value as a Human Being.

Zeros can actually decrease motivation on students, and can quickly destroy them and make them stop caring about their studies altogether.

Once a zero score has been put in the grade book, they need no longer care about that subject and they may assume that, there's nothing they can do about it.

-0-

Author's Profile

Rangeesh Chandrasekar is a MBA Finance and Marketing graduate staying at Chennai. He is passionate about writing and a great lover of books and articles who has Co authored in 800+ anthologies.

rangeeshc1996@gmail.com

08940532223

Reshma Samnani

Destroyed souls do have values

A shop owner placed a sign above his door that said: 'Puppies For Sale.'

Signs like this always have a way of attracting young children, and to no surprise, a boy saw the sign and approached the owner; 'How much are you going to sell the puppies for?' he asked.

The store owner replied, 'Anywhere from $30 to $50.'

The little boy pulled out some change from his pocket. 'I have $2.37,' he said. 'Can I please look at them?'

The shop owner smiled and whistled. Out of the kennel came Lady, who ran down the aisle of his shop followed by five teeny, tiny balls of fur.

One puppy was lagging considerably behind. Immediately the little boy singled out the lagging, limping puppy and said, 'What's wrong with that little dog?'

The shop owner explained that the veterinarian had examined the little puppy and had discovered it didn't have a hip socket. It would always limp. It would always be lame.

The little boy became excited. 'That is the puppy that I want to buy.'

The shop owner said, 'No, you don't want to buy that little dog. If you really want him, I'll just give him to you.'

The little boy got quite upset. He looked straight into the store owner's eyes, pointing his finger, and said;

'I don't want you to give him to me. That little dog is worth every bit as much as all the other dogs and I'll pay full price. In fact, I'll give you $2.37 now, and 50 cents a month until I have him paid for.'

The shop owner countered, 'You really don't want to buy this little dog. He is never going to be able to run and jump and play with you like the other puppies.'

To his surprise, the little boy reached down and rolled up his pant leg to reveal a badly twisted, crippled left leg supported by a big metal brace. He looked up at the shop owner and softly replied, 'Well, I don't run so well myself, and the little puppy will need someone who understands!'"

-0-

Author's Profile

Author name is Reshma Samnani.

Belonging to state of Gujarat. She has been co-author of more than 70 anthologies. She is passionate learner & researcher too. She does work with keen accuracy. She has great management power. She is keen learner of Human Psychology. By profession she is Lawyer. By hobby a writer.

reshmasamnani158@gmail.com

09624710767

<u>**Declaration by Author:**</u>

This is my original content. I have copyright for this write-up & I am providing project head to use it for publishing with my name.

Reshma Samnani, India

Sabita Dakua

Small hopes regained studies

We always heard parents scolding children's from childhood to adulthood with some or other reasons. Here we will understand a childs mistake recorrection in life and a step towards success.

In childhood we were mostly watching cartoons like Tom and Jerry, Scooby-Doo orelse Popeye shows in cartoon network channel. In 90s this shows were popular as well as addiction for small children's. But here a child was spoiled with new daily soap serials of India and started comparing her life with reality.

Once upon a time every child was spoiled and this nut was also from same roots. She has given all her importance in playing and enjoying life with friends. When comes home was occupied with television shows and has maintained distance from studies.

One day mother tried to teach a lesson to this child and has put water in books. She

said from tomorrow you will not go school
and not even out you will be dumped in a
room. Girl was afraid and started crying and
cursing mom for her rude behaviour.

After that she has dried all books and
promised self to score good marks in exams.
She started studies and daily awake till 2am
for revisions. Her board exams came and she
appeared for it with good preparation. As
results were out she passed exams with
distinction. Her mom was so happy to see
the changes and now girl understood what
was the plan behind this punishment.

So, every time parents punish a child for
better results take it positive and react
strongly success will always come back with
your efforts.

Thankyou Mom that girl child was me
unfortunately.

-0-

Author's Profile

Sabita Dakua is passionate about writing and has participated in 15+anthology as coauthor and has compiled 3books.

She handles her writing through Instagram id- @words_clubbed_ and also available at YourQuote app as well as Sabzzwrites page is social page at facebook. She resides at Mumbai, Maharashtra and has completed masters degree. She believes learning should never stop so, restarted studies in psychology. Her hobbies are writing, dancing, listening music, acting, cooking and travelling new places.

sabita.163@gmail.com

8828220385

Declaration by Author:

This is my original content. I have copyright for this write-up & I am providing project head to use it for publishing with my name.

- Sabita Dakua, India

हिन्दी खंड

Alkka Jain

Manacik vikash hetu

बोध्दकि वकिास हेतु अभविादन को सबसे पहले बेहतर साहत्यि उपलब्ध कराये। महापुरुषों की जीवनयिां पढ़ने को दे। शक्षिा का महत्व समझाया जाय। अनुशासन के फायदे बच्चों को बताते जाये। उन्हें नाकारात्मक वचिार से दूर रखा जाये। कसिी जदिगी से हारे हुए पर्दै के हरिो के कस्सिुसे   बजाय वविकानंद साहत्यि दे जो कहता है जतिना बड़ा संषर्ष होगा उतनी बड़ी वजिय प्राप्त होगी।

अपने आप पर वश्विास रखो। असफलता सफलता की पहली सडिी है। आप उन्हीं ओशो साहत्यि भी दे सकते

है परन्तु यह औलाद को बताया जाये कनिर और नारी के वषिय में उनके वचिार हमारी-आपकी संस्कृति से मेल नहीं खाते।दोस्तों पर बालक बालकिओं के भी नजर रखे। वरना सब गुड गोबर हो

सकता है। नशे का चलन आजकल बहुत बड यहा है यदिऔलाद नशा करेंगी तो

बुद्धी नष्ट हो जाती है। एक उपाय है पैसे यानि पोकेट मनी जादा ना दे। रात को १० बजे के बाद घर से ना निकिलने दे। रात को नशे का खतरा अधिक होता हैं।

हर समय औलाद को ना डांटे।

आजकल नेट पर भी अश्ललिता परोसी जाती है। औलाद

को डिस्किवरी चैनल देखने को प्रेरति करें। अश्लीलता ना देखे बच्चे। औलाद को कहें कभी कोई गलती हो जसिमें तो बेझजिक मा- बाप को बताया जाये। कहने का मतलब है किसो दोस्त और एक दुश्मन बराबर होते हैं।यहां दुश्मन याने बुरी आदत से है।एक ग़लत निर्माय जीवन

बर्बाद कर सकता है। निर्णय लेने दे छोटे छोटे ओलाद

को। उसे समझाया जाये कि कानून का उलंघन करना

ठीक नहीं। कानून की जानकारी दी जाये। सेहत ठीक रहेगी तो आदमी बेहतर जिंदगी जी सकता है। नेट पर हो रहे कांड की भी उसे जानकारी दी जाये। सबसे बेहतर है

उसे रोज समाचार पत्र पड़ने की आदत डाले या देखने की समाचार आदत डाली जाये। बताये कि अभी चार अक्षर

पड़ लोगे तो जिंदगी आराम से गुजर जायेगी। चार किताबें कोर्स की पड़े। ये कोई बोझ नही है डिग्री लैना।

ये आपको बेहतर बुध्दि दिती है। से सरि पैर की लड़ाई में ना फंसे। समय का सदुपयोग हो। औलादों के

मनोरंजन का भी ख़्याल रखना चाहिए। दिमाग तरोताजा रहता है।

आजकल बालकों पर बहुत तनाव रहता है अतः मनोरंजन का ख़्याल रखना जरूरी है। दुसरे बच्चों से अपने बच्चे की तुलना नहीं करें। किसी बच्चे को यह ना कहे तुम में अक़्ल नहीं है तुम बुद्धिमान नहीं हो। कहे आज नहीं हुआ कोई बात नहीं अगली बार बेहतर होगा।

अक्सर एक बच्चे को बचपन में नालायक करार दे दिया

जाता है ऐसा ना करें। कभी कभी उस की जिद भी पूरी

करें। अपराधी से दोस्ती ना हो। किस्मत का रोना बच्चों के सामने ना रोये। आखिरि में कहूंगी कि जिरूरत से ज्यादा बच्चे का ख़्याल ना रखें। बजिली टेलीफोन का बलि भरना आदि छोटे मोटे काम

करवाते रहे। हम भारतीयों किआदत रहती है हम बच्चों का जरूरत से अधकि ख्याल रखते हैं जो बालक की बुद्धकिा वकिास नहीं होने देता। साहत्यि आदमी को बुद्धमिान बनाता है

याद रखें सदैव

अलका जैन

-0-

Author's Profile

Alkajain

Birtha place dhar m.p.

Educational bsc

Birthday 8_10 _ 57

Comedian too

 Durdarshan 0ra akashwadi me kavita path

alkajain8888@gmail.com

7806097392

Ankita Dwivedi

12 +12=24

कल काली रात भी आएगी, ये 24 घंटे की सुबह बस
12 बजे तक ही रह पाएगी,

साल में एक दनि ऐसे होते है जब रात बड़ा और दनि
छोटा होता है, तब रात को लगता है की अब वक़्त
उसका है,

और साल में एक दनि ऐसा होता है जब दनि बड़ा
और रात छोटा होता है और दनि को लगता है वक़्त
उसका है,

पर असल में दोनो ये भूल जाते है की वक़्त एक बार
अगर उसका है तो दूसरी बार उसका भी होगा,।

वक़्त अपने सही वक़्त से चलता है कभी कभी हम ही
देर या जल्दी कर देते हैं,

दनि है तो रात होना है।

रात है तो दनि होना हैं।

दोनो 12-12 घंटे का होता हैं,

अब ये जरूरी नहीं की आप अपने उस काम को सुबह के 12 बजे करो।

आप रात के 12 बजे भी कर सकते हो।

और जरूरी ये भी नहीं की आपने अपने काम को 12 बजे रात को करो आप दिन में भी कर सकते हो,

जरूरी ये है की आप उस काम को जब भी करो बस 24 घंटे के अंदर करो,

क्यों की दिन तो आयेगा रात भी आएगा 24 घंटे में और 24 घंटा भी आएगा।

पर वो दिन वो रात और वो 24 घंटा आपका आपको आपके आज के लिए मिला होगा आज के काम को करने के लिए कल के काम को करने के लिए नहीं,।

आपने अपने आज के 24 घंटे को खो दिया अगर, तो आपने अपने जिंदगी के 24 घंटे को खो दिया,   मान

लो और जब आपने अपने जिंदगी के 24 घंटे को खो दिया तो,

आपने अपने मरते वक़्त तक में इस 24 घंटे के खोए काम को नहीं कर पाओगे और यूंही अधूरे काम कर के मार जाओगे, क्योंकी 24 घंटे का जो काम आज करना था,   वो तो आपने कल किया और कल का परसो ऐसे ही चलता है, एक दिन मरने का वक़्त आ गया और आपका आखरी काम अधूरा रह गया,।।

बस 24 घंटे गवाने के कारण आपने अपनी पूरी जिंदगी लगा दी जिस काम को पूरा करने में फिर भी वो अधूरा रह गया,

सर्फि 24 घंटे के वजह से इसलिए तुम काम रात के 12 बजे करो या दिन के बस उसे 24 घंटे के अंदर या 24 घंटे में पूरा करो, समझे,

वैसे ये सवाल अभी भी सवाल ही है ??जवाब है तो दो कोई!!??!!

की 12 बाद 13,14,15,16 ऐसे क्यों नही आते,

अच्छा ये 24 घंटे में 12-12 दो बार क्यों आते है ??

12 के बाद 13,14,15 ऐसे कर कर के 24 तक क्यों नहीं जाते है,??

Ankita Dwivedi ✍️✍️

3:03am

18/12022

AD ✌️

-0-

Author's Profile

This is ankita dwivedi from bihar... Belonging form a small place but with big dreams .....,

Writing is her passion it help her to get connected to her own world of words ...., writing is not just her hobby it's her passion....., ankitadwivedi25771122@gmail.com

6201649115

<u>Declaration by Author:</u>

This is my original content. I have copyright for this write-up & I am providing project head to use it for publishing with my name.

Ankita Dwivedi, India

Archana Kumari

प्रेरणा- एक परिणाम या वरदान

संसार की हर एक चीज प्रेरणा का पात्र है अगर
हम उसमे सक्षमता देखते हों।

फर्श पर बिखरी धूल से लेकर दीवारों और कोनो पर
लगे जाले तक,

प्रेरणा देते हैं की उनकी मौजूदगी ही सफाई का
कारण बनती है।

राह पर चल रहे बंजारों से लेकर महलों में रह रहे
लोगों तक,

प्रेरणा देते हैं की चाहे व्यक्ति गरीब हो या अमीर
एक छत की आवश्यकता सबको है।

गलियों में रहने व भटकने वाले जानवरों से लेकर
पंजिरे मे बंद पंछियों तक,

इस बात की प्रेरणा मिलती है की पालन पोषण की जरूरत केवल नवजात नही मूक जानवरों को भी है।

शहर मे बड़ी बड़ी दुकानों से लेकर गांव की छोटी छोटी गुमटियों तक,

ये बात दर्शाती है की साधन होना कितना जरूरी है।

एक कामयाब इंसान की तरह एक हारा हुआ इंसान भी उतना ही प्रेरणा का पात्र है।

एक कामयाब इंसान की क्रियाओं का प्रशक्षिण कर आप प्रेरणा ले सकते हैं की किस प्रकार किसी काम को अंजाम दे सकते हैं।

वहीं एक हारा हुआ इंसान उम्मीद की किरण लिए नाकामयाबी की दौर में किस प्रकार चलते रहना है, ये सीखा जाता है।

बेहद खुश इंसान सिखाता है की खुशियां समेटने के लिए नही, दिल खोल कर मुस्कुराने के लिए होती हैं।

दुखों से घिरा इंसान सिखाता है की अंधकार में धैर्य
रखने से उजाले का आगाज जरूर होता हैं और
उल्लास की वर्षा भी होती है।

आंसुओं का बहना सिखाता है की दर्द को पनपने की
बजाए बहाना जरूरी है।

असीम आघात के बाद भी अश्रु की धारा का प्रवाह
न होना सिखाता है की कभी कभी आंसुओं का सैलाब
जरूरी नही,

दर्द का एहसास जरूरी है।

सड़क पर भूख से छटपटाता बच्चा एक मनचाहा
भोजन प्राप्त किए व्यक्ति को उसकी खुशकिस्मती
का एहसास दिलाता है।

गली के किसी कोने में एक कंबल ओढ़े व्यक्ति का
चैन की नींद सोना, महल के नर्म बिस्तर पर सो रहे
व्यक्ति को उसकी बेचैनी का एहसास दिलाता है।

तुम मान लो तो हर एक सूक्ष्म चीज में प्रेरणा छिपी है, बात तुम्हारे दृष्टिकोण की है।

प्रेरणा एक परिणाम भी हो सकता है।

प्रेरणा एक वरदान भी हो सकता है।

पर दोनो ही स्तथियियों में प्रेरणा का होना सर्वोपरि है।

-0-

Author's Profile

Archana is an undergraduate student who just loves to write. She is persuing CA and also aspires to be a writer. She loves reading books, novels and stories. You could find her writing something every now and then as it's her daily routine.

archanakri478@gmail.com

6205189478

Declaration by Author:

This is my original content. I have copyright
for this write-up & I am providing project
head to use it for publishing with my name.

Archana Kumari, India

Banaso Kumari

मुसाफिरि बढ़ते चलो। राह में मुस्कलि होगी हजार,तुम दो कदम बढ़ाओ तो सही। मुस्कलि है पर इतनी नहीं की तुम कर न सको। दूर है मंजलि लेकनि इतनी भी नहीं की तुम पा ना सको। तुम चलो तो सही तुम चलो तो सही। तुम दो कदम बढ़ाओ तो सही,हो जाए गा सपना साकार। एक दनि तुम्हार

कोशशि कर, हल नकिलेगा

आज नहीं तो, कल नकिलेगा.

अर्जुन के तीर सा सध

मरूस्थल से भी जल नकिलेगा.

मेहनत कर, पौधों को पानी दे

बंजर जमीन से भी फल नकिलेगा.

ताकत जुटा, हमि्मत को आग दे

फ़ौलाद का भी बल निकलेगा

ज़िंदा रख, दिल में उम्मीदों को

गरल के समंदर से भी गंगाजल निकलेगा.

कोशिशें जारी रख कुछ कर गुजरने की

जो है आज थमा-थमा सा, चल निकलेगा

-0-

<u>Author's Profile</u>

Banaso Kumari is 17 year old student from jharkhand.She love to write.She is free spirit and nature lover.She love to write to express her hidden feelings.She believe that writing is directly connected to heart and is better to express emotions. She have a such a creativity that she can write anything connected to real life and emotions.....she is little sensitive girl,she writes all her poems getting lesson from her life.She is a author of her solo book also...tooo she is co-author in more than 50 books .

banasoku78@gmail.com

6206386923

<u>Declaration by Author:</u>

This is my original content. I have copyright
for this write-up & I am providing project
head to use it for publishing with my name.

Banaso Kumari, India

Jaivir Singh

वो आँगन गुम हो गया

आँगन की वो किलकारियाँ,

गीत बन जाती थी।

दादा-दादी की बातें मिलकर,

संगीत बन जाती थी।

चाचा-ताऊ ने दी आवाज़,

ढोलक की ताल बन जाती थी।

पिता के आते ही,

आँगन में चिल्लाहट मच जाती थी।

सब बच्चों की हाज़िरी,

आँगन में एक साथ लग जाती थी।

अब वो आँगन गुम हो गया,

जहां बच्चों की मस्ती भरी दुनिया होती थी।

शाम ढलते घर के सदस्यों की,

भीड़ लग जाती थी।

सब मलिकर बैठते,

थाली सबकी एक साथ सज जाती थी।

एक चूल्हे पर खाना पकता,

औरतों की फ़ौज लग जाती थी।

आँगन के बीच में बैठे,

घर की बड़ी सबको खाना परोसती थी।

सब मलि कर एक साथ खाते,

ऐसी परम्परा परिवार में होती थी।

अब वो आँगन गुम हो गया,

खाने वालों की जहां जमात लग जाती थी।

खाने के बाद सबकी,

हँसी मज़ाक़ शुरू हो जाती थी।

इस मस्ती भरी महफ़िल में,

छोटे-बड़े सबकी भागीदारी होती थी।

सब अपनी-अपनी सुनाते,

ठहाकों की गुंज आँगन में होती थी।

दिनभर किसने क्या किया,

ऐसी चर्चा एक साथ होती थी।

निद्रा बिस्तर में जाने से पहले,

अगले दिन की तैयारी पे चर्चा होती थी।

अब वो आँगन गुम हो गया,

जहां एक खुशहाल ज़िंदगी होती थी।

भेद-फ़र्क़ की नीति,

कभी देखने को नहीं मिलती थी।

सब में प्रेम भावना की,

ज्वाला जो जलती थी।

छोटे-बड़े सभी में,

आज्ञाकारी बनने की होड़ होती थी।

घर में चौधरी एक होता,

उसके आदेश की तामील होती थी।

एक-दूजें में सम्मान की भावना,

कूट-कूटकर जो भरी होती थी।

अब वो आँगन गुम हो गया,

जहां ज़िंदगी खुलकर मुस्कुराती थी,

-O-

Author's Profile

जयवीर सिंह, शोधार्थी, सावित्रीबाई फुले पुणे विश्वविद्यालय, पुणे

sjaivir21@gmail.com

9860881202

Declaration by Author:

This is my original content. I have copyright for this write-up & I am providing project head to use it for publishing with my name.

Jaivir Singh, India

Mrs. Shashi Prakash

ज़िन्दगी जीने का नाम है

ज़िन्दगी जीने का नाम है,

अरमान अपने रखने हैं ख़ास हमें।

सोच अपनी बदल लेनी है,

जैसे भी हालात हों हमारे।

खुद पर हमेशा भरोसा रखना,

अपनी कमियों पर एक नज़र रखना।

इरादे अपने मज़बूत कर लो,

मंज़िल को अपनी ज़िद बना लो।

विश्वास रखकर अपने दिलों में,

खुद के लिए सच्चे बन जाओ।

हिम्मत ज़रा रख लो,

अपने आप में,एक नज़र मलिा लो।

अपना डर ख़त्म कर लो,

खुद को चाहे पूर्णतः बदल लो।

नींद की दास्तान छोड़कर,

अब वक्त है वक्त के साथ ज़रा चल लो।

अंजाम का डर छोड़कर अब,

आगाज़ सफ़र का जोरों से कर लो।

हाथों की लकीरों को कर्मों से बदल लो,

अपने आप में परिपूर्ण हो लो।

जो खूबसूरत लम्हा मलिा है,

इस लम्हें को तुम लपक लो।

सोच अपनी सबसे जुदा रख लो,

शद्दित से अपने तुम कर्म कर लो।

सारी पीड़ाएं हो जाएंगी बेमानी,

सारी मुश्किलें आसान होंगी।

तुम सफ़र करना की शुरुआत तो कर लो,

काफ़िला खुद ब खुद तैयार होगा।

मंज़िल पर अपनी नज़र टिका लो,

दृढ़ नश्चिय अपने मन में कर लो।

हज़ारों मुश्किलों में भी नहीं रुकोगे,

सफल हो जाओगे ही, यह प्रण कर लो।

-0-

Author's Profile

इनका नाम श्रीमती शशि प्रकाश हैं। इन्हें पढ़ने और लखिने का बहुत शौंक है। कविता लेखन में वशिष रूचि रखतीं हैं। ये अपनी कविताओं के माध्यम से उन सभी भावों को उजागर करना चाहती हैं जो इन्होंने एक बेटी, एक बहन, एक पत्नी और एक मां

के किरदार निभाते हुए महसूस किया है। उस ज़रूरत को समझा है जो कि किसी माध्यम के अभाव में कहीं गुम हो जाती हैं।

pnikitah1974@gmail.com

9548330358

<u>Declaration by Author:</u>

This is my original content. I have copyright for this write-up & I am providing project head to use it for publishing with my name.

Mrs.Shashi Prakash, INDIA

Ms. Pooja Rajesh Nichole

सुपर वुमन

'नौकरी और घर सँभालते हुए बनी सी. ए. ...'

अभी सुनी एक वार्ता है। पता नहीं पर इस वार्ता को सुनकर आनंद से ज्यादा दुःख हुआ। ऐसा नहीं की उनकी प्रगति पर जलन की बात हो, पर बात रखने का रवैय्या कुछ समझ नहीं रहा था। ऐसी बहुत सी बातें हमारा ध्यान अपनी ओर खींचती है। पर इसमें जो बात दबाई गई है वो सभी को नहीं दिखती है। मखमल के वस्त्र में जैसे खंजर रखा हो, वैसा कुछ ऐसी बातों को देख कर लगता है।

स्त्रियों ने शिक्षा लेनी चाहिए, उन्होंने नौकरी भी करनी चाहिए, यह सब बातें समाज करता है। पर यह सब करने से पहले उन्होंने घर को संभालना है, तब ही उनका बाहर जाने का रास्ता खुला होगा, यह नियम क्यों ? यह कौनसा न्याय है ? समानता जिसे कहते है, वह यही है क्या ?

यह तो शुद्ध ढ़ोंग और फ़साने का एक तरीका हुआ। संसार में जितनी जिम्मेदारी स्त्री की है, उतनी जिम्मेदारी पुरुष की क्यों नहीं होती ? कभी थोड़ा ज्यादा ध्यान दे दिया तो उसके पुरुषार्थ को ठेच लग जाएगी क्या ?

हमारे समाज में पहले से कुछ नियम लगाए गए थे, जिनके मुताबिक सब घर परिवार सम्बन्धी कामकाज स्त्रियों को दिए गए है। कामों का कुछ ऐसा विभाजन हमने किया है, किसका अंत क्या ही हो ! इन अनलिखी पर गौर से पाली जाने वाली सभी मान्यताओं का हमारे रहन-सहन पर जो असर हुआ, उसका फिर कभी नाश न हुआ !

स्त्री ने सब काम संभाल कर फिर खुद संभल कर बाकि काम करने चाहिए, यह कल्पना उसे जो नहीं वह आशा दिशा दिखिती है। 'सुपरवूमन' होने का सपना दिखा कर उस से समाज ज्यादा की अपेक्षा लगाए रखता है। और यहाँ सुरु होती है उसकी कसरत

! स्त्री के बारे यह 'सुपरवूमन' की संकल्पना न जानते हुए उनका नाश करती है। हमें जैसे हमारे हक़ पता होते है, वैसे ही हमें अपने कर्त्तव्य भी पता होने ही चाहिए। मूलतः इतने उच्च आदर्श विचारों को रखने वाले हमारे देश में इन सीधे बातों पर गौर किया नहीं जाए तो अचरज तो होगा ही ! इन सभी में, आज के हालत में स्त्रियों की होने वाली अनास्था उनकी बलाद्ग्रहण के लिए जिम्मेदार है। घर के सभी कामों का ठेका केवल स्त्री ही क्यों ले ?

आदमि काल में शारीरिक कमजोरी के कारन हो या मातृत्व जैसी जिम्मेदारी के वजह से हो, स्त्री घर संभालती थी और पुरुष शिकार करता था, उस वजह से स्त्री घर पर रहती थी और पुरुष बहार की दुनिया देखता था। आगे बहुत दिन तक यही चलता रहा। बाकि देशों में इन बारे में कुछ बदलाव हुए नजर आते है, पर हमारे 'संस्कृति संवर्धक' देश में अभी भी कुछ बदलाव नहीं दिखाई देते है। इस सभी बातों को शायद कुछ पुरुष 'फेमनिज्म' की दृष्टि से देखेंगे। पर

'फमिल' होने के लिए पहले 'ह्यूमन' होना जरुरी होता है, यह शायद सब लोग भूल गए है।

अपेक्षाओं के बोझ तले 'शारीरकि तौर पर कमजोर स्त्री को और भी कमजोर बनाई जाती है। क्या गलत हो जाएगा अगर पुरुष ने उसे ज्यादा नहीं पर कभी खो सके उतनी ही मदद कर दी ?

एक ही प्रकार का काम करने पर भी घर आने के पुरुष को चाय-नास्ता लगता है। स्त्री पहले सब बनाए, उसको हाथ में दे। फरि खाने का देखे, घर के काम नपिटाए, बच्चों पर ध्यान दे, घर के बुजुर्गों क्या ख्याल रखे और क्या काम न करे ! घर पर वैसे तो दोनों ही थक कर आते है। पर वो सब भूल कर फरि काम में लग जाती है। उसकी 'सेकंड शफ्िट' अभी बाकि ही होती है ! इन सब में कब रात और फरि सुबह कब होती है, इसका ध्यान उसको भी नहीं रहता। और है छुट्टी के दनि तो सब हफ्ते की तैयारी करना एक बड़ा काम हो जाता है।

स्त्रियों को पढाके हमने उन पर जतिने 'उपकार'
किये है, उससे ज़्यादा तो 'सुपरवूमन' की अपेक्षा
रख हम उन पर अन्याय कर रहे है, कुछ गलत बोल
रही हूँ क्या ?

आखिरि क्या, तो घर हो या दफ़्तर, उसकी छुट्टी
होना असंभव है, यह एक मथ्यिा कल्पना है।

ऐसा नहीं है, की सभी पुरुष या सभी घरों में ऐसा
अनुचति व्यवहार करते है। कुछ लोग ऐसे भी है, जो
अपनी धर्मपत्नी की इस कदर इज़्जत करते है के
देखने लायक है, देखने क्या, उनका अनुकरण करने
जैसा है। दूर क्यों जाना, मैंने ऐसे लोग देखे है। यह देख
लगता नहीं के यह सच्चाई है, पर ऐसा भी होता है।
पर ऐसे लोग बहुत काम है। कुछ ज़्यादा ही पुण्य
कमाने पड़ते होंगे ऐसे जीवनसाथी पाने के लिए ! पर
क्या होगा, अगर सभी लोग ऐसे समझदार नकिले,
और हाँ, क्या होती है स्त्री ? एक शब्द में कहे तो
'फीलग्सि' ! आप अगर थोड़ा प्यार का, सम्मान का,

कदर का हाथ बढ़ाएंगे, तो वो खुद ही आपको कुछ करने ना दे ! बस एक बार उसको अपनी बना कर तो देखे, उसका दर्द समझकर तो देखे। पर इसका मतलब ये भी नहीं की इस 'निजा टेक्नकि' का इस्तेमाल आप गलत तरीके से काम से बचने के लिए करे।

इसलिए ये जो सृष्टि के दो पहिय है, वह ऐसे ही बस एक दूसरे के साथ ही नहीं, तो एक दूसरे का साथ पा कर यह जीवन पार करे, और बाकि लोगों के सामने आदर्श प्रस्थापति करे, यही छोटी सी आशा है ...

और हाँ, बाकि चीजों के बारे में ज्यादा सोचने की जरुरत नहीं है, क्यों की, वो स्त्री है, कुछ भी कर सकती है...

-0-

Author's Profile

Writer is a Research Fellow of English working in Dept. of English, JDMVP's Art's,

Commerce and Science College, Jalgaon
affiliated to Kavayitri Bahinabai Chaudhari
North Maharashtra University, Jalgaon. She a
transcendental writer having her own blog:
poojanichole.blogspot.com.

She writes on various platforms like Pratilipi,
Bluepad and Yourquote Apps. She is a
versatile writer who writes in English, Hindi
and Marathi.

poojanichole@gmail.com

8805507244

Declaration by Author:

This is my original content. I have copyright
for this write-up & I am providing project
head to use it for publishing with my name.

Ms. Pooja Rajesh Nichole, India

Neelaksh

कैसे प्रेरक निबंध लोगों को यह महसूस करने में मदद करते हैं कवि क्या हैं ?

चार मुख्य प्रकार के निबंध हैं: तर्कपूर्ण, व्याख्यात्मक, कथात्मक और वर्णनात्मक। प्रेरक निबंध आमतौर पर 'कथा' श्रेणी के अंतर्गत आते हैं। ऐसा इसलिए है क्योंकि वे किसी विषय की इतनी खोज या विश्लेषण नहीं कर रहे हैं क्योंकि वे कुछ करने के पीछे के कारणों पर चर्चा कर रहे हैं। वे अभी भी एक तर्क प्रस्तुत करते हैं, लेकिन यह अक्सर एक अकादमकि के विपरीत एक व्यक्तगित तर्क होता है।

प्रेरक निबंध अक्सर अन्य प्रकार के निबंधों की तुलना में शैली और स्वर दोनों में कहीं अधकि व्यक्तगित होते हैं। उदाहरण के लिए; एक अंग्रेजी साहित्य कार्यक्रम के संदर्भ में एक तर्कपूर्ण

नबिंध। एक तर्कपूर्ण नबिंध दो अलग-अलग ग्रंथों की तुलना, विपरीतता और विश्लेषण करेगा।

एक प्रेरक नबिंध, इस बीच, ग्रंथों के बारे में आपके व्यक्तिगत दृष्टिकोण पर चर्चा करेगा किआप उन्हें क्यों पसंद करते हैं या नापसंद करते हैं, और आपने उन्हें पढ़ने से क्या हासिल किया या नहीं किया। प्रेरक नबिंध आमतौर पर अधिक व्यक्तिगत स्वर पर प्रहार करते हैं। अन्य प्रकार के नबिंधों के विपरीत, वे आपके और आपके विचारों और विचारों के बारे में अधिक हैं।

-0-

Author's Profile

Neelaksh hails from Lucknow, Uttar Pradesh. He has completed his B.com from Jai Narayan pg college and is pursuing Chartered Accountant. He usually writes as a part of his hobby. He express himself beautifully and love to write on different occasions . He

always tries to bring smiles to everyone face..
He is always hopeful and bring positive
memories to others

neelakshca97@gmail.com

+917565830357

<u>Declaration by Author:</u>

This is my original content. I have copyright
for this write-up & I am providing project
head to use it for publishing with my name.

Neelaksh, India

Omprakash Kshatriya Prakash

लेख- विचारों का स्वास्थ्य पर प्रभाव

ओमप्रकाश क्षत्रिय 'प्रकाश"

एक छोटी सी कहानी है, आप ने भी सुनी होगी. एक लकड़हारा था. लकड़ी काट कर बेचता था. यही उस की आजीविका का साधन था. एक दिन जब वह लकड़ी काट रहा था तो किसी जीव ने उसे काट लिया. उस ने हाथ को झटका दिया. काटा होगा किसी ने, यह सोच कर उस ने पेड़ के खोखले में पत्थर का टुकड़ा घुसेड़ दिया.

10 वर्ष बीत गए. लकड़हारे का जीवन उसी तरह चलता रहा. इस दौरान वह पेड़ सूख गया. एक दिन लकड़हारे ने वही पेड़ काटा और उसे कुल्हाड़ी से फाड़ने लगा.

इस दौरान पत्थर पेड़ से छिटक गया. वह दूर जा गिरा. लकड़हारे को उस खोखले में सांप का ढांचा

दिखाई दिया. यह देख कर लकड़हारा सन्न रह गया. उसे 10 साल पहले की घटना याद आ गई.

लकड़हारा सोचने लगा, '10 वर्ष पहले मुझे सांप ने काटा था. उस का जहर मेरे खून में चढ़ा था और मैं आज तक जिंदा हूं. कहीं वह जहर मेरे खून में तो नहीं घूम रहा है?'

यह सोचसोच कर लकड़हारा घबरा गया. उसे ठंड के मौसम में भी पसीना आ गया. वह सीधा घर गया. तब से वह बीमार रहने लगा. फरि एक दनि वह मर गया.

लकड़हारा जहर से नहीं मरा था, जहर के भय ने उस के प्राण हर लिए. सब से पहले मस्तष्कि में उथलपुथल मची. उसे महसूस हुआ कि खून में जहर आज भी दौड़ रहा है. इसी वचिार से उस कि शक्ति क्षीण होने लगी. उस के पाचन संस्थान ने काम करना बंद कर दिया. इस से खून में श्वेत रक्त

कणिकाओं की संख्या घटने लगी और अंत में वह मर गया.

कई लोग इसी तरह विचारों की तीव्रता से अपनी जान गंवा देते हैं. उन्हें कहीं कोई बीमारी नहीं होती है. अत्यधिक खुशी या गम उन के मस्तष्कि में तीव्र वेग से विचार उत्पन्न कर देता है जिस का शरीर पर तुरंत प्रभाव पड़ता है. शरीर मस्तष्कि में उठे बवंडर को स्वास्थ्य पर संभाल नहीं पाता है. परिणामस्वरूप शरीर के कमजोर स्थल पर अवरोध उत्पन्न हो जाता है. इसी कारण वे असमय ही काल के ग्रास बन जाते हैं.

हम जैसा सोचते हैं, शरीर पर वैसा ही प्रभाव पड़ता है. हम निराशाजनक बातें सोचते हैं तो शरीर पर हानिकारक प्रभाव पड़ता है. सफलता और उन्नति की बातें सोचने से शरीर पर आशाजनक व उत्साहवर्द्धक और निश्चिति प्रभाव पड़ता है.

शरीर क्षीण, दुर्बल, कमजोर और बेकार हो तो भी
विचारों के झंझावातों से उस में शक्ति आ जाती है.
भले ही वह व्यक्ति वर्षों से बीमार हो, पलंग से उठ
नहीं पाता हो तो भी विचारों की तीव्रता उसे
भलाचंगा कर देती है.

इसे हम एक उदाहरण द्वारा समझ सकते हैं. एक
वृद्धा लंबी बीमारी से ग्रस्त थी. वह चलफिर नहीं
सकती थी. कभी पलंग से नीचे नहीं उतरी. ऐसी
अवस्था में एक बार उस के बहू बेटे बाहर गए. उस
वक्त वृद्धा और उस का पोता घर में थे. अचानक
घर में आग लग गई. पोता आग से घिर गया. उस के
सामने मौत नाचने लगी. बचने की कोई संभावना
नहीं थी. वृद्धा चिल्ला पड़ी. वह खूब चिल्लाई पर
आसपास कोई नहीं था, जो उस बच्चे को बचाता.

वृद्धा के पास कोई उपाय नहीं बचा, उस के दिमाग
में विचारों का बबंडर उठ रहा था. अचानक उस ने
निश्चय किया, 'मैं बच्चे को नहीं मरने दूंगी.' यह

सोचते ही वृद्धा की नसों में खून दौड़ने लगा. वह उठ बैठी. वह दौड़ कर गई. आग में घुसी. बच्चे को उठा कर बाहर आ गई. जब वह सामान्य हुई तो अपनेआप को देख कर उसे घोर आश्चर्य हुआ. वह स्वयं चलफिर सकती थी.

उस वृद्धा में शक्ति कहीं बाहर से नहीं आई थी. वह उस के अंदर थी. उसे विचारों ने बल दिया. उस के मस्तिष्क ने उसे चेताया. 'बचा ले, तू बचाना चाहती है तो अपने पोते को, वरना उसे कोई नहीं बचाएगा और वह मर जाएगा.'

इसी विचार से उस के रक्त में विद्युत का संचार हुआ और वह दौड़ कर बच्चे को बचाने में सक्षम हो गई. वृद्धा की सक्षमता कहीं नहीं, उस के विचारों में बसी थी. यही क्षमता हम सब में है. बीमार व्यक्ति विचारों के बल पर स्वस्थ हो सकता है. यही कारण है कि कई ग्रामीण लोग गंगा जल पीने मात्र से स्वस्थ हो जाते हैं.

इन ग्रामीणजनों के स्वस्थ होने का राज उन का अपना विश्वास होता है. उन्हें गंगा जल पर अंधविश्वास है. वह उस के पीते ही स्वस्थ हो जाएंगे, यह मान्यता उन के मस्तिष्क में जम कर बैठी रहती है. फलत: गंगा जल पीने से वे कई बार स्वस्थ हो जाते हैं.

गंगा जल कोई औषधी नहीं है कि उस के पीने से हर कोई स्वस्थ हो जाए. मगर विश्वास, आस्था की दृढ़ता और शरीर की क्रिया इस में महत्त्वपूर्ण भूमिका निभाती हैं. वे शीघ्र ठीक हो जाते हैं.

इसी विश्वास के कारण व्यक्ति नीमहकीम, ओझा और तंत्रमंत्र से ठीक होते देखे जाते हैं. उन तंत्रमंत्र, नीमहकीम और ओझा के पास कोई शक्ति नहीं होती है, न ही उन की दवा, झाड़फूंक काम करती है. व्यक्ति के स्वयं के विश्वास और उस से उपजे विचार ही उसे स्वास्थ्य लाभ देते हैं.

शरीर विचारों का दर्पण है. यह वही व्यक्त करता है जैसा विचार दिमाग या मस्तिष्क में चलता है. बीमार व्यक्ति को देखिए. वह कमजोर, कांतिहीन और कुरूप दिखाई देता है. वहीं प्रसन्न और सफलता से खुश किसी व्यक्ति को देखिए. उस के चेहरे की चमक, शरीर की स्फूर्ति, उत्साह व जोश देखने लायक होता है. यह सब कहीं से नहीं आता है. शरीर एक ही है.

उस पर कोई बाहरी प्रभाव उतना नहीं पड़ता है जितना आंतरिक प्रभाव. यही वजह है कि एक स्थिति में व्यक्ति अपने को स्वस्थ महसूस करता है, दूसरी स्थिति में अस्वस्थ और बीमार.

बीमार व्यक्ति के स्वास्थ्य सुधार की रफ्तार उस के विचारों पर निर्भर करती है. एक सफल, प्रसन्नचित्त व्यक्ति उसी तीव्रता से ठीक होता है जिस तीव्रता से उसे सफलता, प्रसन्नता महसूस होती है.

इस के ठीक विपरीत निराशावादी व्यक्ति को ठीक होने में ज्यादा समय लगता है. ऐसे व्यक्ति का स्वास्थ्य सुधार उस की मनोदशा पर निर्भर करता है.

लता ने यह प्रयोग द्वारा सिद्ध किया है कि हमारे विचारों से हमारे स्वास्थ्य पर सकारात्मक व नकारात्मक प्रभाव भी पड़ता है. लता ने एक बार जीते हुए सैनिकों को सेवासुश्रूषा की थी. उस ने देखा कि जीत की खुशी से उल्लसित सैनिकों के घाव शीघ्र भर गए, जबकि हारे हुए सैनिकों के घाव देर से भरे

इस का कारण उन की अपनी विचारधारा और मनोदशा थी जिस ने उन के शरीर को उसी अनुरूप ढाल दिया था. जीते हुए सैनिकों में उत्साह था. वे सोच रहे थे कि उन का श्रम सार्थक हो गया. वे जीत गए. अब वे शीघ्र स्वस्थ हो कर जीत का जश्न मनाएंगे. फलत: वे शीघ्र ही ठीक हो गए.

इसी के विपिरीत हारे हुए सैनकि नरिाशा से ग्रस्त थे. उन्हें ग्लानकिा अनुभव हो रहा था. वे सोच रहे थे किवे हार गए. अब न जाने कब ठीक होंगे ? इसी कारण वे देर से ठीक हुए. इन सब बातों से यही पता चलता है किहम जैसा सोचते हैं, शरीर के स्वास्थ्य पर वैसा ही प्रभाव पड़ता है. इसलिए हमें अपनी सोच को सकारात्मक बनाना चाहिए ताकिहम स्वस्थ, प्रसन्न और सफल व्यक्तत्वि के स्वामी बन सकें.

ओमप्रकाश क्षत्रयि 'प्रकाश', पोस्ट ऑफसि के पास, रतनगढ़, जलिा-नीमच (मध्यप्रदेश)-458226

-0-

Author's Profile

ओमप्रकाश क्षत्रयि प्रकाश

opkkshatriya@gmail.com

9424079675

<u>Declaration by Author:</u>

This is my original content. I have copyright for this write-up & I am providing project head to use it for publishing with my name.

- OMPRAKASH KSHATRIYA PRAKASH, India

Pooja Mishra

क्यों रुक जाएँ

क्यों रुक जाएँ

क्यों थम जाएँ

अभी तो मंज़िल को पाना है

आगे हमें बहुत जाना है

रास्ते इतने आसन नहीं

बाधाएँ तो आयेंगी

उनसे भी तो टकराना है

फ़ौलादी इरादों से

हमें आगे को बढ़ते जाना है

इतनी सी बाधाओं से

हमको नहीं घबराना है

© Dilettante Pooja Mishra ✍️

-0-

Author's Profile

My Name is Pooja Mishra, I was born & brought up in Ballia UP And for the last 11 years I have been living in Delhi NCR. I have done MCA from UPTU and I have 4 years worked experience and my last company was Tata Business support services. I wrote my first poem when I was in 3rd standard but due to lack of time I was not able to write it. Then again I started writing my poetry from 2020. Now I give my full attention to writing all my time.

poojamshr5@gmail.com

8743895737

Declaration by Author:

This is my original content. I have copyright for this write-up & I am providing project head to use it for publishing with my name.

Pooja Mishra, India

Tejashvi Tripathi

इंतजार का ये खेल जब अपना अंजाम लेगा

इंतजार का ये खेल जब अपना अंजाम लेगा

जब हर कोशिश इन अंधेरों से लड़कर घुटने टेकेगी

जब उम्मीद का नन्हा दिया बुझा के धुआं हो जाएगा

जब मैं अनंत हीरो की खाई में गिर कर खो जाऊंगी

मेरा अस्तित्व भी जब मुझे एक वहम सा लगेगा

जब दूर दूर तक ना रास्ता दिखेगा और न कोई
मंजलि

जब न साथ होगी कोई चाह ना कोई हराह

तब एक सुनहरे वक्त के धक्के से

सूरज का पहिया घूमेगा और अपनी जगह पर लेगा

तब उतरेगी एक रोशनी

होगी एक धूप मेरे हिस्से में भी

दस्तक देगी एक नई सुबह मेरे घर की दहलीज पर भी

-0-

Author's Profile

I'm Surbhi Tripathi from up 52. I usually write in my free time as it's my hobby. For quotes and all things you can follow me on instagram @surbhiii.04

vandanatripathi374@gmail.com

9005597380

Declaration by Author:

This is my original content. I have copyright for this write-up & I am providing project head to use it for publishing with my name.

Tejashvi Tripathi, India

Vaishnavi Suthar

।।तू आगे बढ़।।

तू रुक मत, तू राह बना,

तू आगे चल और हौसला रख,

तू आकाश को छूने की तमन्ना रख,

और कदम बढ़ा,

निराश ना हो और उठ,

तू आगे बढ़ और हौसला रख,

तेरी मंजिल तेरा इंतजार कर रही है,

हां कांटे हैं राहों में,

पर उस दर्द को भूल,

और आगे बढ़,

आजाद पंछी है तू आकाश का,

जसि उडना है पूरे आसमान में,

तू राह बना अपनी,

और आगे बढ़,

तू जदि रख और भरोसा कर रब पर,

तू रुक मत, आगे बढ़,

तू राह बना और चल,

ओर जति अपनी मंजलि को,

तू चल और आगे बढ़।।।।

-0-

<u>**Author's Profile**</u>

Vaishnavi is a 20 year old girl from rajasthan,she works in 15 anthologies already,she is a model by profession and actor,now pursuing bachelor of science, she love to do dance,painting,travelling and reading,reading and writing is something she live everytime and spend her day well with books she love to experiment new things,she love to do yoga and motivate people who are suffering from depression and stress she believe a healthy body do everything with positive mind,this motivational poem I dedicate to all the people who want to chase their dreams and working hard every single day,hope you enjoy, and keep loving and keep reading .

Instagram = Vaishnavi. Suthar.

Facebook =Vaishnavi suthar.

Snapchat =Vaishnavi suthar.

vaishnavisuthar28@gmail.com

9079024404

<u>Declaration by Author:</u>

This is my original content. I have copyright for this write-up & I am providing project head to use it for publishing with my name.

Vaishnavi Suthar, India

Vijay Singh Raj

पूरेरणा

हौसला यदि है अगर, मंजलि न तेरी दूर है

रास्ता हो दूर कितना, मंजलि न तेरी दूर है

सितारों को पाने की हसरत, लेकर उड़े थे तुम अगर

पा ही जाओगे सितारे, हौसला यदि है अगर

सोचते क्यों मन में तुम हो, मैं ऐसा कर सकता नही

सोच कर इक बार देखो, जो किए तुममें से ही

सीखना यदि चाहते, सीख सकते हो अभी

वक्त का क्या भरोसा, अब नही तो कभी नही

देख कर चींटी की हस्ती, भर लो तुम विश्वास को

वो तो है नन्ही सी चींटी, तुम तो इक इंसान हो

देखकर आईने को अगर तुम, संवारते हो खुद को अगर

एक गलती से सीख लो, सीखना चाहते हो अगर

पत्थर को इक बार देखो, चोट से डरता नही

चोट से डरता अगर वो, मूरत बन सकता नही

वक़्त का पहिया, धरातल पर कभी रुकता नही

पा ही लूंगा खुद की मंजिल, अब तो मैं रुकता नही

वजिय सिंह राज

-0-

<u>Author's Profile</u>

My self Vijay singh raj form Kanpur Nagar. I have Post graduate with hindi my hobby write poem and story. My write many poem and story

singhvijay1889@gmail.com

09936330756

<u>Declaration by Author:</u>

This is my original content. I have copyright
for this write-up & I am providing project
head to use it for publishing with my name.

Vijay Singh Raj, Kanpur

आशीष पाण्डेय

दहेज़ प्रथा का अन्त कैसे हो?

दहेज प्रथा समाज में उसी प्रकार है जैसे सोने के बीच में कोयला। और हर मनुष्य उस कोयले के पीछे भखारियों की तरह दौड़ता हुआ दिखाई दे रहा है सच कहूं तो दहेज प्रथा संचालन करने वाली स्वयं औरत है जो दहेज के साथ आती है और दहेज के साथ लाती है।

औरत यदि न चाहे तो दहेज प्रथा का कोई महत्व नहीं रह जायेगा यदि औरत अपने बेटे के लिए मांग न करे तो दहेज प्रथा समाज में नाम मात्र रह जायेगी और हर गरीब अपनी बेटी का विवाह शान से कर सकेगा। दहेज प्रथा को बंद करने के लिए स्वयं औरतें ही नारा लगाती हैं और औरतें ही दहेज के लिए पीड़ित करती हैं उस प्रकार जैसे समुद्र अपने अन्दर अग्नि पैदा कर पाले हुए जीवों का संहार करता है उस प्रकार स्त्री भी नारा लगाकर स्वयं

दहेज के लिए पीड़ित करती है। दहेज समाज में नमक की तरह घुल गया है जिससे मुक्त होने के लिए स्वयं घोलने वाले को संभलना होगा और इसे रोकना होगा यदि नारी समाज चाहे तो आज़ ही दहेज प्रथा का अन्त हो सकता है किन्तु वो चाहती नहीं वो तो स्वयं चाहती है दहेज प्रथा और वृद्धि करे इसीलिए तो अपने आप को नहीं सुधारती है और न ही दहेज के मना करती है एक दो के मना करने से दहेज प्रथा का अन्त नहीं होगा दहेज प्रथा का अन्त करने के लिए सारी नारी समाज को संकल्प बद्ध होना पड़ेगा तभी दहेज प्रथा का शमन हो सकता है अन्यथा नहीं। नारी दहेज की आग में जल चुकी है लेकिन समय आने पर वो भी दूसरी नारी को दहेज की आग में जलाने के लिए तत्पर रहती है दहेज प्रथा लागू किसने किया कहां से हुई मैं नहीं जानता लेकिन इतना जानता इसे बढ़ावा नारियों के लालच ने दिया है कहीं कहीं पुरूषों का हाथ अधिक मात्रा में रहा है लेकिन ज्यादातर नारियों ने स्वयं दहेज प्रथा को बढ़ावा दिया है यदि

लड़के की मां घर वालों से ये कह दे की मुझे दहेज नहीं लेना है लड़की के पिता से लड़की के अलावा और कुछ नहीं चाहिए तो ऐसा कोई नहीं जो नहीं मानेगा सब मानेंगे, कोई कोई लज्जाहीन होगा जो नहीं मानेगा लेकनि आज की नारी स्वयं हाथ पसारे बैठी रहती है कि कब कोई आये और मैं उसे दहेज रूपी कुल्हाड़ी से हलाल करूं। नारी यदि दहेज के लिए मना कर दे तो पुरुष दहेज नहीं लेगा और दहेज प्रथा का अन्त हो जायेगा। वरना ये विष सदियों से घुल रहा है और लोग इसके प्रभाव से जल रहें हैं और जलते रहेंगे। नारियों को अब जागृत होना चाहिए ये सोंच कर की उनकी भी कोई बेटी है और इसी तरह मैं भी हलाल की जाऊंगी। जसि दनि नारी ने ये संकल्प ले लिया उसी दनि दहेज़ प्रथा का अन्त हो जायेगा। बेटियों के मां बाप शौक़ से अपनी बेटी का वविाह करेंगे और वो खुश रहेगी लोग अपनी अपनी हैसयित के अनुसार अपनी बेटी का वविाह अपने बराबर या अपने से कम या ज़्यादा दौलत वाले के यहां वविाह कर सकेंगे।

दहेज़ प्रथा समाप्त हो जायेगी। नारी जिस दिन यह विचार बनाकर कार्यरत हो जायेगी दहेज प्रथा छू मंतर हो जायेगी। वरना ये अग्नि जलती रहेगी लोग जलते रहेंगे।

आचार्य आशीष पाण्डेय

-0-

Author's Profile

आचार्य आशीष पाण्डेय १२-७-२०००-सुल्तानपुर उत्तर प्रदेश के परसडा नामक ग्राम में हुआ है इनकी बचपन से ही काव्य में रुचि रही जिसके फलस्वरूप इन्होंने २० वर्ष की अवस्था में पुस्तकों की रचना की, विभिन्न पत्रिकाओं में इनकी रचना प्रकाशित हुई है और आगे भी होती रहेगी।ये काव्य भारती, सरस्वती सृजन सम्मान,युवा,शक्ति, सरदार वल्लभ भाई पटेल जैसे आदि पुरस्कारों से सम्मानित हैं

ये अभी अध्ययन रत है और भागवत कथा
कर्मकाण्ड,ज्योतिषि आदि के जानकार भी हैं

ashishpandey70005@gmail.com

07355982747

<u>Declaration by Author:</u>

This is my original content. I have copyright
for this write-up & I am providing project
head to use it for publishing with my name.

आशीष पाण्डेय, India

भावना वधिानी

समझौता

हमारे जन्म लेते हैं ही हमारे साथ कई रिश्ते जुड़ जाते हैं जैसे माता-पिता भाई बहन दादा दादी चाचा चाची मौसा मौसी नाना नानी। जैसे जैसे हम बड़े होते हैं हमको इन सब रिश्तो से मधुर व्यवहार बनाए रखना पड़ता है। हमारे यह रिश्ते हाथों की अंगुलियों की तरह होते हैं जो एक ही हथेली से जुड़े होते हैं परंतु सबका अपना स्वतंत्र व्यक्तित्व होता है। सबका अपना एक अलग स्वभाव होता है। सब की अलग अपनी रुचियां अलग शौक होते हैं। हमें अपनी जिंदगी में इन रिश्तो को बनाए रखने के लिए कभी-कभी किसी बात में या किसी भी हालात में कई समझौते करने पड़ते हैं जिनके लिए हमारा दिल गवारा नहीं होता परंतु फिर भी रिश्तो की मर्यादा को बनाए रखने के लिए हमें वह समझौते करने ही पड़ते हैं। हम अपनी जिंदगी में जितनी भी समझौते

करते हैं उसमें भले हमारी खुशी शामिल ना हो परंतु जिंदगी को व्यवस्थित रूप से चलाने के लिए और रिश्तो की गरिमा को बनाए रखने के लिए हमें समय-समय पर अपने मन को मारकर भी कई समझौते करने पड़ते हैं और हम करते भी हैं। जो लोग अपने जीवन में परिस्थितियों लोगों रिश्तो के साथ समझौता नहीं करते वो हमेशा दुखी और परेशान रहते हैं। इसलिए अपने अहम को दरकिनार कर अगर सब की भलाई के लिए हमें किसी भी बात में समझौता करना पड़े तो कर लेना चाहिए। पर जहां बात अपने आत्मसम्मान अपने स्वाभिमान की आती है वहां पर किसी भी प्रकार का समझौता नहीं करना चाहिए।

सौ, भावना विधानी @bhavnavidhani123

-0-

<u>Author's Profile</u>

अमरावती निवासी सौभाग्यवती भावना मोहन कुमार वधानी को बचपन से ही लेखन का बहुत शौक रहा है। उन्होंने अपने लेखन का सफर कक्षा सातवीं से बाल कविताओं के रूप में शुरू किया। उन्होंने अब तक काफी सारे लेख शायरी कहानियां कविताएं लिखी है, जो काफी सारी पत्र-पत्रिकाओं में प्रकाशित हो चुकी है। उन्होंने कई बार ऑनलाइन कवि सम्मेलनों में भाग लिया है। लेखन के साथ-साथ भावना जी को बागवानी कुकिंग और गायन का शौक है। भावना जी ने शादी से पहले सहायक शक्षिका के रूप में भी कार्य किया है। भावना जी को सोशल वर्क में भी बहुत रूची है। वो अमरावती की कई सामाजिक संगठनों से जुड़ी हुई हैं। उन्होंने अपने घर में एक छोटा सा किचन गार्डन बना कर रखा है उनका मानना है कि सबके घरों में पेड़ पौधे होने चाहिए।

bhavnavidhani7@gmail.com

7507000651

शेख़ शहज़ाद उस्मानी

शेष कुशलमंगल है

बाप रे! सोचा न था कि इस वाली रोमांचक यात्रा में इतनी सारी मुसीबतों का सामना करना पड़ेगा! अकेला चला था, कारवाँ बनता गया। कोरोना... कोरोना नाम मलिता गया। मेरे आक़ाओं की क्या मनशा थी, क्या मंसूबे थे... सचमुच मुझे पता नहीं! मुझे अपने मंसूबे भी पता नहीं थे। मैं तो सबके साथ अपने वकिास की ओर चल रहा था अपनी वरिासत को सँभालता हुआ। लेकनि सच कहूँ... बहुत मज़ा आया और आ रहा है आज भी। खलिाड़ियों को लोकप्रयि मोबाइल गेम-जी में भी कभी उतना रोमांस और रोमांच महसूस नहीं हुआ होगा, जतिना मुझे चाइना के वुहान से यूरोपीय देशों और साउथ-ईस्ट के देशों की यात्राओं में महसूस हुआ। मज़े लेने के लिए यक़ीनन बेशरम, ढीठ, जुल्मी, तानाशाह, हत्यारा सब कुछ बनना पड़ता है अपनी स्टेज

डविलप करने के लिए उन मोबाइल गेम-जी की
तरह। पॉइंट्स हासिल करता जा रहा था मेरे
मुक़ामात और मानव-मौतों के आंकड़ों के रूप में! कहीं
स्टेज-1 पर था, तो कहीं स्टेज-2 पर, तो कहीं
आक़ाओं की क़ामयाबी की बुलंदियों को छूती तीसरी
स्टेज पर! इस दौरान के पूरे अनुभव अपने इस
संस्मरण में लिखूंगा, तो मानव-मौतों के आंकड़ों
वाली संख्या में यह आलेख हो जायेगा।

सच कहूँ! मानव के शरीर को मैंने स्मार्ट-फ़ोन सा
महसूस किया। आंतरिक शरीर को हार्डवेअर;
हथेलियों को की-पैड। हरक़तों-गतिविधियों को
कमांड और सोच-विचारधाराओं और आदतों-
प्रवृत्तियों को सॉफ़्टवेयर-ऐप्लकिशन्स!

मेरे साथ व्यवहार के नियम उन देशों के ज़िम्मेदार
लोग नागरिकों को समझा ही रहे थे मुझे वापरने,
त्यागने या हराने बावत!

लेकनि मज़े की बात यह है कि मानव की यह
विशेषता मुझे साक्षात नज़र आई कि ग्रंथों-पुराणों,
संविधान-क़ानूनों और शैक्षणकि पाठ्यक्रमों में जो
कुछ भी उसे सिखाया-पढ़ाया जाता है न, मानव उन्हें
अपने नजी क़ायदे-क़ानूनों में ढाल कर या मिश्रित
कर अपने स्वार्थ पूरे करता है। जहाँ तक मेरी बात
है, मेरे धर्म-कर्म की बात है, उसे समझने के लिये
मानव के पास स्थानीय चकित्सिक, नेता, अधिकारी,
पुलसि-सेना, एनजीओ आदि के अलावा 'हू' ही है।
अरे, वही WHO जो दुनयिा भर की जानकारी देकर
दुनयिा भर की ज़िम्मेदारियाँ नभिाया करता है, वही
'हू', बस! शेष प्रश्नवाचक शब्दों वाला कोई नहीं
दुनयिा के मानवों के पास! न व्हाट, व्हाइ, व्हेन,
हाऊ और न ही व्हिच या हूम। न तो हाऊ मेनी, हाऊ
मच और न ही हाऊ लाँग!

इन सब के जवाब बेचारा WHO ही देता जा रहा था
मेरी धांसू रोमांचक यात्रा संदर्भति और उसी की
तर्ज पर हर देश की सरकार, मंत्री-संतरी या

शक्षिक और स्वास्थ्य-रक्षकगण! लेकिन मानव
भी क्या ग़ज़ब की चीज़ है! सबके साथ, सबकी सुनता
और समझता है, लेकिन करता वही है, जिससे
शॉर्टकट से उसके तात्कालिक स्वार्थ पूरे होते हैं
अपने निजी नियमों और क़ायदे-क़ानूनों पर चलकर
और थोपे गये वालों पर चलकर उपेक्षा, अवज्ञा या
अवहेलना करके! दरअसल मानव विभिन्न
आपदाओं, दंगों-फसादों, युद्धों और महामारियों में
इतना मौत-तांडव देख, सुन, पढ़ या देख चुका है कि
मौत से डरकर भी अब डरता नहीं है। मेरे गेम में मौत
के भयावह आंकड़ों के समाचार सुनकर डर भी रहा
था और हॉरर मूवी माफ़िक़ मज़े भी ले रहा था या
मुझसे और मेरी रोमांचक गतिविधियों से संबंधित
विभिन्न विधाओं में भला या भोंडा साहित्य-सृजन
कर रहा था या स्मार्टफ़ोन के तथाकथित लोकप्रिय
ऐप्लिकेशन्स से दिलचस्प या फूहड़ सृजन कर
आत्म-सुख या पर-सुख महसूस कर रहा था।

लेकिन इन सब बातों का चश्मदीद गवाह बनता हुआ
अपने अड्डे बदलता हुआ अपने अनजाने-अनचाहे
और अपने आक़ाओं के मनचाहे अनलमिटिडि सफ़र में
कभी नवीन कारवाँ बनाते हुए, तो कभी साथियों की
शहादत बरदाश्त करते हुए अनजानी दिशाओं में
बढ़ता ही चला जा रहा था।

अपनी विश्ववव्यापी यात्राओं के दौरान पड़ाव-
ठहराव हेतु बड़ी मुश्किल से अपने घोंसले और
आशयिाने बना पा रहा था। कहीं-कहीं मुझे फाइव
स्टार होटल जैसा सुख मिला, तो कहीं भारत की
सड़कों, हाट-बाज़ारों या नालयिों-गटर जैसा। लेकिन
हर जगह चुनौतियाँ थीं मेरे जीवन, मेरे अस्तत्त्वि
और विकास के समक्ष। सजग मानव बार-बार बीस-
बीस सैकंड तक हथेलियाँ-कलाइयाँ धो रहे थे साबुन
या सेनीटाइज़र्स से। सतह रूपी मेरे हर संभव
मुक़ामात और आशयिानों पर नाना प्रकार से हमले
हो रहे थे। जीना मुश्किल हो रहा था। मैंने खुद को

और अपने कारवाँ को कैसे बचाया, मैं सीमित शब्द-
संख्या में बयाँ नहीं कर सकता।

वो तो मेरे आक़ाओं की बदौलत मेरा कारवाँ बनता
जा रहा था। कभी बिखरता या मिटता भी था, तो हम
में से कोई न कोई एकला चल पड़ता था, चढ़ पड़ता
था मानव शरीर में और फ़िर... फ़िर से एक कारवाँ
बन जाया करता था।

अपनी अँखियन देखी और दुनिया के दुखियन की
सीमित शब्दों में बयाँ करना बहुत ही मुश्किल है।
लेकिन मौक़ा मिला है, समय भी मिला है और लेखनी
भी चल पड़ी है, सो कुछ तो कह कर रहूँगा ही।
आख़िरि मानवों ने मुझे और मेरे कारवाँ को बहुत तंग
जो किया है।

अपनी यात्राओं में दुनिया में मौजूद हर आम
यातायात वाहनों में मैंने 'सफ़र' और 'सफर' किया है।
हवाई जहाज़, रेलगाड़ी, बसों, दोपहिया वाहनों में...
हर माध्यम से। मानवों के हाथ मिलाने की परम्परा

से लेकर, उनकी चीख, छींक, खांसी, लार, थूक और वस्त्रों आदि की सतहों से मानव के गले, आंतों, लीवर, किडनी वग़ैरह की भव्य तफ़री करना पर्यटन सा आनंद दे रहा था। सच कहूँ, तो मैं उस दरम्यान स्वयं को शोधकर्ता पर्यटक समझ रहा था या अपने आक़ाओं के अंडर में कोई शोधकर्ता या वैज्ञानिक! कितने नज़दीक़ से मानव के शरीर को, उसकी आदतों को, उसकी मज़बूरियों-विवशताओं, तानाशाही और गुलामियों को मैंने समझा है। राजा हो या रंक, मालिक हो या सेवक, नेता हो या मतदाता! उनके अज़ीज़ों, क़रीबों, रिश्तेदारों, चिकित्सकों, सेवकों और सुरक्षाकर्मियों ... सबके हलक़ से गुज़र कर मैंने बहुत से शोध किये हैं अपने आक़ाओं की शैली में; मेरे घोंसले या आशयिाने रूपी बीमार मानव की मौत के पहले और मौत के बाद! उसके चौदह दिवसीय आइसोलेशन की अवधि में, उसके पहले और फ़िर उसके बाद! उफ़्फ़! ओह, आह, अँय!

बाप रे! ऐसा भी होता है इस जगत में! अपना भी अपना नहीं रह जाता! सोचा न था कि इस वाली रोमांचक यात्रा में इतनी सारी हक़ीक़तों और मुसीबतों का सामना करना पड़ेगा!

अब मेरे पास अधिक समय नहीं है। आक़ाओं के मशिन पर मुझे आगे यात्रा करनी है। सो, केवल एक घर का एक क़िस्सा ही सुना रहा हूँ।

मैं गीताबाई की हथेलियों पर सवार था उस समय, क्योंकि वह विदेश से लौटे, मेरे साथी कोरोना से संक्रमित उस रईसज़ादे के घर पर रसोई का काम निबटा कर आई थी, जिसने अपनी कोई जाँच नहीं करवाई थी। उसके घर पर उसका अय्याश बाप ही था, कोई महिला नहीं थी। मैं स्वयं को सुरक्षित करते हुए अपना कारवाँ बढ़ाने वास्ते गीताबाई के साथ हो लिया था। अब वह एक दूसरे रईस परिवार के बँगले पर झाड़ू पोंछा करने जा रही थी। अच्छी खासी सोसाइटी थी। यहाँ मेरे लिए बड़ा स्कोप था।

बंगला नंबर 7K के मुख्य द्वार पर उसने कॉलबेल देर तक बजाई। अंदर से बहस सुनाई दी।

"कौन आया है इस कर्फ़्यू के वक़्त!"

"काम वाली आई होगी! तुमसे तो कुछ होता नहीं, तो आज मैंने उसे बुला ही लिया! सरकारी नियम से तनख़्वाह तो देना ही पड़ेगी न!"

"लॉकडाउन और कर्फ़्यू की ऐसी-तैसी कर दोगी तुम तो! लगता है ज़ल्दी मरना चाहती हो कोरोना वाइरस से!"

"सुबह-सुबह उस कमीने वाइरस का नाम क्यों ले रहे हो! आज करवा लेते हैं उससे झाड़ू-पोंछा! कल से नहीं आयेगी!"

इसके साथ ही दरवाज़ा खुला। गीताबाई अपसेट हो गई थी।

"मुझे थोड़े न कोरोना हुआ है! हर कोई मना कर रहा है घर में आने को! हद है!" मन ही मन में बड़बड़ाते

हुए उसने इरादतन दरवाज़े के हैंडल पर दो-चार जगह हाथ लगाकर अंदर से दरवाज़ा बंद कर दिया।

 उसने बैठक में सोफ़े पर अपना स्मार्ट फ़ोन रख दिया और फैले सामान को व्यवस्थति कर झाड़ू लगाने की तैयारी कर रही थी। मेरा कारवाँ अपने अड्डे बनाता जा रहा था। लेकनि मैं बहुत भयभीत था उसकी हथेलियों में। तभी उसने अपनी नाक खुजाई। मैं तुरंत ही उसकी नाक में शफ्टि हो गया। तभी मालकनि गीताबाई को वॉश-बेसनि के पास ले गई और हैंडवॉश से उसके हाथ धुलवाने लगी। लेकनि मेरा कारवाँ तो लगभग उसके पूरे शरीर पर अड्डे बना चुका था पछिले वाले बंगले में।

मालकि गीताबाई की हर एक गतविधि पिर नज़र रखे हुए थे। गीताबाई झाड़ू लगाने लगी। फ़रि सभी कमरों में झाड़ू-पोंछा सम्पन्न हुआ।

मालकि, मालकनि को इशारे से डांट रहे थे। मालकनि बुरा सा मुंह बनाकर उन्हें इशारों में लकीर का फ़कीर

आदर्शवादी कह कर चढ़ा रही थीं। यह सब गीताबाई ने भी देख लिया था। अब उसकी आँखों से आँसू छलक पड़े।

मालकि का ध्यान पोंछा लगाती गीताबाई के माँसल शरीर से उसकी भीगी आँखों पर पहुंच गईं।

मैं भी दुखी सा उसकी नाक और मुंह में शफ़्टिंगकी कोशिश कर रहा था बेहतरीन मुक़ाम हासलि करने के लिए।

"क्यों रो रही हो? घर में किसी को कोरोना तो नहीं हो गया?" मालकि ने गीताबाई से हमदर्दी जताते हुए पूछा।

"नहीं भाईसाहब! सब घर में बैठे रोटी तोड़ रहे हैं दो महीनों से! सब ठीक हैं! भगवान की कृपा है हम ग़रीबों पर!" गीताबाई का ये जवाब सुनकर मैं कैसा महसूस कर रहा था, बयाँ नहीं कर सकता।

लेकिन तभी मालकि के कड़क स्वर मुझे सुनाई दयि।

"घर में सबको सब बातें समझाती रहना ज़ालमि कोरोना वाइरस के बारे में! हाथ धुलाई वगैरह सब, जो सरकार बता रही है। ..और हाँ ..कल से मत आना। फ़ोन करें, तभी आना दो महीने बाद। हम पूरी तनखाह देते रहेंगे, चिंता मत करना!"

यह सुनकर गीताबाई मालकिन की ओर देखकर ज़ोर से रोने लगी। फिर दोनों हथेलियों से उसने अपने आँसू पोंछे और फ़िर पोंछा पूरा कर मोबाइल उठा कर वापस जाने लगी।

उसने ज़ोर से दरवाज़े का हैंडल घुमाया जानबूझकर झुंझलाहट में और चली गई।

मालकि ने तुरंत सेनेटाइज़र की बोतल उठाई और उस सोफ़े पर, झाड़ व पोंछे पर कुछ बूंदें उड़ेलीं और फ़िर कॉलबेल पर भी!

तभी मालकिन चीखीं :

"क्या सेनेटाइज़र इसी के लिए लाई थी मैं ख़रीद कर!
पूरा ख़त्म कर दोगे इतना महंगा वाला! तुमसे
ज़्यादा समझदार, सफ़ाई पसंद और क़ायदे वाली है
गीताबाई!"

अब मैं क्या करता। मेरा काम भी पूरा हो चुका था।
मेरा कारवाँ तरक़्क़ी पर था, अपने अड्डों पर था।

ऐसे एक नहीं, लाखों अनुभव हुए हैं मुझे नाना प्रकार
के मेरे कारवाँ की बरबादी और बढ़ती आबादी दोनों
के।

वास्तव में मुझे गर्व है अपने और अपने आक़ाओं के
विकास पर, सफ़ल मशिन पर। लेकिन एक दुख भी है!
वो यह कि कुछ लोग मुझे कोवडि-19 या सार्स कॉव-
19- 2 कहते हैं, तो अधिकतर केवल कोरोना! कुछ
लोग मज़ाक में मुझे 'करो न... करो ना!' कहते हैं,
जबकि कुछ संवेदनशील मुझे 'करुणा' कह जाते हैं। हर
देश की क्षेत्रीय भाषाओं में मुझे कोई और नाम अब
तक तो नहीं मिला! ख़ैर, अपना काम आगे बढ़ता रहे,

बस। डर लगता है कि कहीं मानव इतना समझदार न हो जाये कि मुझे और मेरे कारवाँ को अपने नियंत्रण में ले ले! मैं अपने पूर्वजों से यही कहूँगा कि मेरे समक्ष मानव की कुछ एक चुनौतियाँ हैं, शेष कुशलमंगल है।

शेख़ शहज़ाद उस्मानी

-0-

Author's Profile

दमोह (मध्यप्रदेश) में जन्मे वर्तमान में शिवपुरी(मध्यप्रदेश) के स्थायी निवासी शेख़ शहज़ाद उस्मानी एक अशासकीय शिक्षक (पीजीटी), लेखक, आकाशवाणी नैमित्तिक उद्घोषक, रेडियो नाट्यस्वराभिनिय कलाकार, यूट्यबर, आर.जे., फेसबुक ब्लॉगर, पोडकास्टर आदि रूप में जाने जाते हैं। आप की मुख्य लेखन विधा लघुकथा विधा है। आप हाइकु और अन्य शैलियों में

काव्य लेखन और गद्य लेखन में भी कलमकार हैं। आप की लघुकथायें, हाइकु और अन्य रचनायें विभिन्न प्रतिष्ठित पत्र-पत्रिकाओं, साझा संकलनों व स्टोरी मिरर और ओपनबुक्सऑनलाइनडॉटकॉम आदि वेबसाइट्स पर प्रकाशित हो चुके हैं। आप दिशा प्रकाशन के विश्व हिंदी लघुकथाकार कोश व निदेशिका में भी नामांकित व प्रकाशित किये.जा चुके हैं। आप वीडियो लघुकथा/हाइकु/काव्य पाठ भी करते रहते हैं। फेसबुक पर आपके द्वारा संचालित लघुकथा पाठ/हाइकु पाठ/काव्य पाठ(जनसंचार; जनमंथन) समूह व पेज हैं और यूट्यब पर चैनल भी (sheikh's language and literature zone) - शीघ्र ही आपके निजी एकल संग्रहों के प्रकाशन की योजना है।

sheikh.shahzad.usmani.lekhani.lekhani@gmail.com

9406589589

<u>Declaration by Author:</u>

This is my original content. I have copyright
for this write-up & I am providing project
head to use it for publishing with my name.

शेख़ शहज़ाद उस्मानी, India

Anamika

एक संघर्ष सपनों की उड़ान का ...

मणिपुर नामक गांव में भीमसेन अपनी पत्नी सीला और दो बेटियों संगीता और गीता के साथ रहते थे।

संगीता उसकी बड़ी बेटी थी और गीता छोटी बेटी थी, भीमसेन बहुत गरीब था।

वो बस अपने परिवार के खाने भर का ही कमा पाता था भीमसेन खेती करता और जो फसल होती थी उसे बेचकर वो अपनी बेटियों की फीस भरता था।

ये देखकर संगीता बड़ी दु:खी होती थी, और सोचती थी की मैं बड़ी होकर डाक्टर बनूगीं , मगर गीता पापा के साथ खेत में जाती थी, तो भीमसेन उसको समझाते थे की तुम बड़ी होकर देश की सेवा करना और बॉर्डर पर रहकर देश की सुरक्षा करना, ये सुनकर गीता बहुत खुश हो जाती,और मन में यही

सोचती थी की मैं बड़ी होकर अपने पापा का सपना पूरा करूंगी और भारतीय सैन्य दल में भर्ती लूंगी।

समय बीतता गया और अब दोनों बेटियों बड़ी हो चुकी थी,

भीमसेन को अब उनकी शादी की चिन्ता सताने लगी यह देख सीला बहुत दुःखी होती है।

इधर संगीता की तबयित खराब हो जाती है, जिसके कारण भीमसेन ने जो रात दिन मेहनत करके पैसे कमाये थे वो खत्म हो जाते है, और घर में खाने का राशन भी कम हो जाता है भीमसेन मन में यही सोचता है की बस इस बार की फसल अच्छी हो जाये तो सब ठीक हो जायेगा। उधर सीला यही सोच रही है की अब संगीता और गीता का महाविद्यालय में दाखिला भी करवाना है और पैसा नहीं है,

"कैसे होगा और क्या होगा " यही चिन्ता सीला कमजोर और

बीमार कर रही थी मगर इसकी खबर भीमसेन को नहीं थी।

दोनों बेटियाँ भी अपनी पढ़ाई को लेकर चन्िता में रहती थी। दोनों घर में ही मेहनत और लगन से पढ़ रही थी।

कुछ समय तक सब ठीक चल रहा था, मगर एक रात मौसम खराब हो गया और घनघोर बारिश और ओले पढ़ गये, भीमसेन जब सुबह उठा तो देखा की बारिश हो गई है

तो वो दौड़ता हुआ खेत पर गया और देखा और सर पर हाथ रखकर रोने लगा, क्योंकिबारिश और ओले के कारण उसकी फसल पूरी तरह खराब हो चूकी थी।

भीमसेन को कुछ समझ नहीं आ रहा था बस अपनी बेटियों की पढ़ाई के बारे में सोचकर रो रहा था और बोल रहा था

की अब मेरी बेटियाँ कैसे आगे पढ़ेगी और मेरा सपना कैसे पूरा होगा।

उसके मन में यही ख़्याल आ रहा था कि अब सब बरबाद हो गया है मेरे पास कुछ नहीं रहा," मैं कैसे घर जा कर बोलूंगा और क्या बोलूंगा "।

उसने मन में सोचा की मुझे कुएँ में कूद कर मर जाना चाहिए, अब जीने के लिए कुछ नहीं बचा है।

यही मन में सोचकर भीमसेन मरने जा रहा था, जब वो कुएँ के पास पहुँचा और कूदने ही वाला था की आवाज आयी की, "अरे भीमसेन तू ये क्या कर रहा है, तूने ये सोचा की तेरे मरने के बाद तेरी पत्नी और तेरे बच्चों का क्या होगा"।

भीमसेन ने जब ये आवाज सुनी तो वो रूक गया और इधर उधर देख रहा था की बोल कौन रहा है आवाज किसने दी

मगर कोई नजर नहीं आया, तभी उसने शान्त होकर सोचा

तो पता चला की ये आवाज तो उसके अंतर आत्मा की थी जो उसे ऐसा करने से रोक रही थी, तभी उसके सामने सीला और दोनों बेटियों का चेहरा सामने आ गया और वो रूक गया भीमसेन ने अपने आँसू पोछे और घर वापस लौट आया।

घर आते ही उसने अपनी दोनों बेटियों को गले से लगा कर रोने लगा और बोला की मुझे माफ कर दो मैं बहुत बड़ा पाप

करने जा रहा था ये देख सीला भी रोने लगी।

सीला बोली हम और मेहनत करेंगे खूब पैसा कमायेंगे और अपनी बेटियों को पढ़ायेंगे, ये बोल कर सीला कमरे में चली गई।

दुसरे दिन सीला बाहर जा रही थी तो भीमसेन ने पूछा की आज कुछ त्योहार है क्या, तो सीला बोली

नहीं मैं काम पर जा रही हूँ ताकी अपनी बेटियों को पढ़ा सकूं।

सीला दूसरों के घर जाकर बर्तन और पोछा करने लगी,

और भीमसेन सेठ जी के घर मजदूरी करने लगा।

सीला जिस घर में काम कर रही थी उसी घर की मालकनि ने पूछा की सीला तुम इतनी मेहनत क्यों करती हो तुम्हारी तो दो बेटियाँ है, तुमको आराम करना चाहिए और तुम्हारी बेटियों को काम ये सुनकर सीला बोली की नहीं मालकनि मेरी बेटियाँ पढ़ाई कर सके इस लिए ही हम और इनके पापा मेहनत करते है मुझे पता है की वो बड़ी होकर हमारा नाम ही नहीं वो इस गाँव का नाम भी रौशन करेंगी , इतना बोलकर सीला अपने घर चली आयी आज सीला के चेहरे पर एक मुस्कान थी और मन में वश्विास।

सब कुछ ठीक चलने लगा, संगीता और गीता भी मेहनत करके पढ़ रही थी, और महाविद्यालय में टॉप कर रही थी,

कठनि परश्रिम के बाद आखरि एक दनि उनकी मेहनत रंग लायी,जब वो अपने पापा का सपना पूरा करके के घर लौटी, भीमसेन और सीला की आँखों में खुशी के आँसू थे और गाँव के लोग भी यही बोल रहे थे की मुझे पता था किआपकी बेटियाँ एक दनि आपके नाम के साथ साथ इस गाँव के नाम को भी रौशन करेंगी।

Anamika singh

<u>Author's Profile</u>

I am a writer I am fond of writing story and poetry, I want to be a successful writer and want to reach my poems to the people, I consider my words my identity. I do not compare myself with anyone, whatever I write from my heart I write

anamika6924@gmail.com

9335199858

<u>Declaration by Author:</u>

This is my original content. I have copyright for this write-up & I am providing project head to use it for publishing with my name.

Anamika, India

Kiran Kumari

तिरंगे की शान

मैं बन प्रहरी, सरहद पे हूं खड़ी,

सीना तान।

माटी में ही बसी है,मेरी जान।

मैं हूं भारत की बेटी,

मैं भी बढाऊंगी,तिरंगे की शान।

सुनती आई हूं,वीरो का किस्सा।

मैं भी जियूँ, उनका हिस्सा,

भीगी पलकों में,करके बसेरा,

 तुमने तो बदला डेरा,

याद आते हो,तुम वीर महान।मैं बन प्रहरी, सरहद पे हूं खड़ी,

सीना तान।

माटी में ही बसी है,मेरी जान।

मैं हूं भारत की बेटी,

मैं भी बढाऊंगी,तरिंगे की शान।

सुनती आई हूं,वीरो का कसि़सा।

मैं भी जियूँ, उनका हसि़सा,

भीगी पलकों में,करके बसेरा,

 तुमने तो बदला डेरा,

याद आते हो,तुम वीर महान।

 तुझसे ही है तरिंगे की शान।

मै भी बढऊंगी,तरिंगे की शान।

सदी बदल रही है,बदल रहा है,

ये जमाना,ना बदली है,

वीरो की कहानी,ये आज भी,

हंसते-हंसते देश पे,लुटाते जवानी।

शत शत नमन,वीर जवान।

तुझसे ही है,तरिंगे की शान,

मैं भी बढाऊंगी तरिंगे की शान।

तुझसे ही है तरिंगे की शान।

मै भी बढऊंगी,तरिंगे की शान।

सदी बदल रही है,बदल रहा है,

ये जमाना,ना बदली है,

वीरो की कहानी,ये आज भी,

हंसते-हंसते देश पे,लुटाते जवानी।

शत शत नमन,वीर जवान।

तुझसे ही है,तरिंगे की शान,

मैं भी बढाऊंगी तरिंगे की शान।

-0-

<u>Author's Profile</u>

नाम -करिण कुमारी

शिक्षा -एमएससी बॉटनी ऑनर्स

स्थान -जमशेदपुर

कुशल गृहणी।

kirankumarii1979@gmail.com

9608484679

<u>Declaration by Author:</u>

This is my original content. I have copyright for this write-up & I am providing project head to use it for publishing with my name.

Kiran kumari, INDIA

Mr. Umaji Subhash Patil

वारसि

रामप्रसाद का बेटा - अक्षय अमरिका क्या चला
गया,बस वही का होकर रह गया । वही गृहस्थी बसा
ली । रामप्रसाद यहा अकेला, पत्नी को गुजरे सालो
हो गए । घर-गृहस्थी संभालते-संभालते थक गया
बेचारा । अब हाथ-पावो ने भी साथ देना छोड दिया ।
ले-दे के बस सहारा है,तो बस एक दोस्त तुलसीराम
का ।वही तो उसको चार दिन पहले धर्मादाय
अस्पताल मे भरती कर के गया था । लो वह आ गया,
"रामप्रसाद ! कैसी है सेहत अब ?"

"अब आराम जरुर है, पर बुढ्ढे को जवान तो नही
किया जा सकता ।"

"सो तो है,उम्र का तकाजा ..."तुलसीराम ने
कहा,"तुम्हारी देखभाल तो ठिक से हो रही है यहा ?"

"घर मे अकेले पडे रहने से तो बेहतर है कि मेरा यहा कोई देखभाल तो करता है । यहा की डा. नयन ने मेरी खूब देखभाल की ।बिल्कुल एक बेटी की तरह मेरा खयाल रखती है ।"

तुलसीराम सोचता रहा-'क्या बताऊ दोस्त ..... डा.नयन वही तेरी बेटी है, जो वारसि (बेटे) की चाहत मे तुने मेरे हाथो अनाथालय मे भेजी थी ।आज सब के होते हुए,सभी अनाथ.....'

-0-

<u>Author's Profile</u>

पूरा नाम- श्री उमाजी सुभाष पाटलि

माता का नाम - अक्काताई पाटलि

पतिा का नाम - सुभाष पाटलि

जन्म तथि- 03/06/1985

व्हाट्स ऐप न० - 8459772723 / 8698957793

ई-मेल पता - patilumaji@gmail.com

शैक्षकि योग्यता - एम.ए., एम.फलि.(हिंदी), NET
(UGC-NTA, हिंदी)

उपलब्धियाँ-

1.राष्ट्रवाणी(द्वैमासकि, अकं 6,मार्च-अप्रैल
2012) में 'डा.राज बुद्धरिाजा के उपन्यासो में नारी
' शोध-पत्र

प्रकाशति

2.अतंर्राष्ट्रीय शोध पत्रकिा आयुषी(फरवरी
2020) में 'डा.राज बुद्धरिाजा के कावेरी उपन्यास में
नारी समस्याएँ' शोध-पत्र प्रकाशति

3.रंगमचं प्रकाशन द्वारा प्रकाशति
'रामकाव्य'(साझा काव्य सकंलन) में कवतिा
सकंलति

4 प्रज्ञांजली(2006)मेंआलेख ' उपन्यास सम्राट प्रेमचदं ',कविता 'प्रिया',पहेलियाँ प्रकाशति

5. चिंतन साहित्यिकि एवं सांस्कृतकि संस्था द्वारा आयोजति प्रेमचदं जयंती समारोह 2020 में कहानी पाठ।

6.आजाद-ए-हिदं, साहित्य पीठ सम्मान 2020, उत्तर प्रदेश सद्भावना सम्मान, वागीश्वरी सम्मान, महाराष्ट्र

गौरव सम्मान, साहित्यवीर, महाराष्ट्र कोहनिूर,काव्य केशर, आदि35 से अधकि सम्मान से सम्मानति

7.150 सेअधकि संगोष्ठीयों में सहभागिता

8. 50 से अधकि प्रश्नोत्तरी में सहभागिता

पूरा पता- चरण,तहसलि-शाहूवाडी, जिला-कोल्हापुर (महाराष्ट्र)416213

patilumaji@gmail.com

8698957793 /8459772723

<u>Declaration by Author:</u>

This is my original content. I have copyright for this write-up & I am providing project head to use it for publishing with my name.

Mr. Umaji Subhash Patil, India

Nobel Shriwas

संयुक्त परिवार

यह कहानी शहर से काफी दूर एक गांव की है,गांव में चार भाई रहते थे,क्रमशः उनका नाम राम,बलराम,राधेश्याम, घनश्याम, था, राम सबसे बड़ा था, राम की शादी होते ही उसने अपना परिवार अलग कर लिया,एवं शहर में जाकर रहने लगा,वही बलराम अपने दोनों भाइयों एवं माता पिता के साथ रहने लगा, घर की सारी जिम्मेदारी बलराम पर आ गया बलराम ईमानदार, मेहनती था,बलराम ने अपनी पढ़ाई रोक कर काम करने लगा एवं अपने दोनों भाइयों को घनश्याम एवं राधेश्याम को पढ़ाने लगा, बलराम खेती किसानी करता था और अपने घर परिवार का पालन पोषण करता था,कुछ दिनों बाद बलराम भाइयों की पढ़ाई पूरी होने के बाद उनका शादी करता है और खुद भी शादी कर लेता है,

दोनों भाइयों की पत्नियों पढ़ी लखिी थी परंतु
बलराम की पत्नी अनपढ़ थी, बलराम की पत्नी
दोनों देवर को अपने बेटों के समान तथा देवरानयिों
को अपनी बहन के समान समझती थी, मंजलिं भाई
घनश्याम ने शहर में अपना खुद का व्यवसाय शुरू
कयिा,वही छोटे भाई राधेश्याम को,शहर में प्राइवेट
कंपनी में नौकरी मलि जाती है, उनकी पत्नियों के
बोलने पर, राधेश्याम और घनश्याम,बलराम से
अलग होने की बात करता है,

बलराम की लाख समझाने पर भी नहीं मानते,और
अपना- अपना परविार लेकर के शहर चले जाते हैं,
अब बलराम फरि से अपनी पुरानी दनिचर्या, सुबह
गाय के लिए चारा लाना,दनि भर मेहनत मजदूरी
खेती बाड़ी का काम देखना, ऐसे ही बलराम का
जीवन शांतपिूर्वक अपने पत्नी एवं नशिक्त माता-
पतिा के साथ गुजर रहा था,

वहीं दूसरी ओर घनश्याम को व्यवसाय में भारी
नुकसान हुआ, बड़ी मुश्किल से उसका घर चल पाता
था,तथा छोटे भाई राधेश्याम का एक एक्सीडेंट में
एक हाथ टूट चुका था इसलिए राधेश्याम को नौकरी
से निकाल दिया गया, राधेश्याम को खाने तक के
वांदे हो गए थे,किंतु दोनों भाई बलराम के पास जाने
के लिए संकोच कर रहे थे,किसी तरह बलराम को इस
बात का पता चला, तो वह स्वयं अपने दोनों भाइयों
के पास आकर उन्हें गले से लगा लेता है, और
समझाने लगता है सब ठीक हो जाएगा, दोनों भाई
बलराम के पैरों में गिर कर फूट-फूट कर रोने लगते हैं,
बलराम उन्हें फिर से अपने घर चलने को कहाता है,

 राजी खुशी तीनो भाई अपने गांव के घर में चले जाते
हैं,तथा खुशी -खुशी जीवन व्यतीत करते हैं,

समाप्त

वर्तमान में छोटा परिवार सुखी परिवार के चक्कर
में लोग अपना-अपना घर अलग कर रहे हैं,

याद रखिए आपका परिवार ही आपकी ताकत है

-0-

Author's Profile

Noble shriwas

janjgir-champa chhattisgarh

Bajaj financer field officer

graduate completed

nobelshriwas766@gmail.com

9630218667

Declaration by Author:

This is my original content. I have copyright for this write-up & I am providing project head to use it for publishing with my name.

Nobel shriwas, India

Rahul Sharma

Love story ❤, यादगार तस्वीरें इस दुनिया की

#.Love story ❤

1. Tere Bina Tutkar Bikhar Jayenge,

Tum Mil Gaye To Gulshan Ki Tarah Khil Jayenge,

Tum Na Mile To Jite Ji Mar Jayenge,

Tumhe Paa Liya To Markar Bhi Jee Jayenge.

@rahul_sharma

2. Udas nahi hona kyon ki main saath hoon,

Saamne na sahi par aas-paas hoon,

Palkon ko band kar jab bhi dil mein dekhoge,

Main har pal tumhare sath hu!

@rahul_sharma

3. Ishq mohabbat to sab karte hai,

gam-a-judai se sab darte hai,

hum to ishq karte ha na to mahabbat,

hum to bas aapki ek mushkurahat pane ke liye taraste hai.

@rahul_sharma

4. कुछ हदें हैं मेरी कुछ हदें हैं तेरी..!!

लेकनि दायरों में भी इश्क़ होता है…!!❤

@rahul_sharma

#. यादगार तस्वीरें इस दुनिया की

1. सफ़र की हद है वहां तक की कुछ निशान रहे,

चले चलो की जहाँ तक ये आसमान रहे।

ये क्या उठाये कदम और आ गयी मंजलि,

मज़ा तो तब है के पैरों में कुछ थकान रहे।

वो शख़्स मुझ को कोई जालसाज़ लगता हैं,

तुम उसको दोस्त समझते हो फरि भी ध्यान रहे।

मुझे ज़मीं की गहराइयों ने दबा लयिा,

मैं चाहता था मेरे सर पे आसमान रहे।

अब अपने बीच मरासिम नहीं अदावत है,

मगर ये बात हमारे ही दरमयिान रहे।

सतिारों की फसलें उगा ना सका कोई,

मेरी ज़मीं पे कितने ही आसमान रहे।

वो एक सवाल है फरि उसका सामना होगा,

दुआ करो कसिलामत मेरी ज़बान रहे।

@rahul_sharma

2. अपने हस्सिे का सारा ग़म लेकर बैठे हैं

धूप अधकि हम छांव बहुत कम लेकर बैठे हैं

खचिकर आते हैं सारे ग़म हँसती आँखों से

सो अपनी ये दो आँखें नम लेकर बैठे हैं

दर्द सजा सकता है खुशियाँ हमको पता चला

जैसे ही हाथों में रेशम लेकर बैठे हैं !

सारे छोड़ गए हैं हमको किसी बहाने से

जबसे हम ये दुख का परचम लेकर बैठे हैं

एक नया मौसम जागा है लेकर अँगड़ाई

और अब तक हम बीता मौसम लेकर बैठे हैं !

हमको अपनी तन्हाई से शिकवा नहीं रहा

जबसे कागज़ और क़लम हम लेकर बैठे हैं !

@rahul_sharma

-0-

<u>Author's Profile</u>

Myself Rahul sharma. I from in maihar,
Madhya Pradesh. I read in b. Com with (C.A)
2nd year . My hobby in writing and

technology field . My biggest dream in technology engineering.

atlasit9179@gmail.com

7354575975

<u>Declaration by Author:</u>

This is my original content. I have copyright for this write-up & I am providing project head to use it for publishing with my name.

Rahul Sharma, India

Usha

पतिजी

कहानी तो मेने बहुत सुनी कुछ परियों की तो कुछ अनजानों

की,कुछ कहानियां जंगल के जानवरों की।

पर यह जो मे बताने जा रही हूं,यह न तो परियों की है ना जंगल की।

यह तो मेरे जीवन को प्रेरणा देने वाले मेरे पतिजी की है।

जिन्होंने कभी भी हार नहीं मानी, उस जमाने मे एक बेटी

का जन्म लेना अखरता था,फिर हम तो छःबहने ही थी।

भाई न था फिर भी हमें अहसास नहीं होने दिया कि हम

लड़कियाँ है।

हाथ में साइकिल लिए पीछे एक बैग रखा हुआ, साधरण से दखिने वाले,मेरे पतिाजी गेट मे आकर घंटी बजाकर अपने आने का संकेत देते | हम जल्दी से अपनी कितीबे लेकर बैठ जाते, सभी शांत हो जाते |

सबसे पहले पतिाजी का बाहर रखा सामान देखना सब ठीक ठाक है,तरीके से रखा गया है या अव्यवस्थति।

जरा सा भी इधर उधर हुआ देखते तो पहले उसे ठीक करना,फरि बैठकर आराम से तांबे के लौठे में रखा पानी पीते थे, उसके बाद कुछ खाते थे।

यदि हमारा सामान खराब देखते तो हमारी शामत थी।

पढ़ाई के प्रतिलापरवाही उन्हें पंसद नहीं थी।

पिताजी को स्वच्छता से रहना व सब जगह स्वच्छ रखना अच्छा लगता था, अभी भी वह घर को व्यवस्थित व स्वच्छ रखना पंसद करते है।

पिताजी एक अध्यापक थे जो अब रिटायर हो चुके है।

स्वाभिक था हमारा शिक्षा के प्रति रूझान, पिताजी ने हम सब

को बीए एम ए कराया व रुचिनुसार मेरी दीदी को कम्प्यूटर कोर्स भी कराया व छोटी बहन को प्रभाकर की उपाधि दिलवायी।

मेने भी बीए एम व शादी के बाद बीएड वहीं से किया।

पिताजी ने कभी नहीं सोचा कि दुनिया क्या सोचती है?

मां का भी सहयोग करते थे जैसे छोटे में हमारे बाल बनाना,

हमारे बस्ते(beg) लगाना, हमारे पढ़ाई का सारा इंतजाम पिता□जी करते थे, पिताजी एक अध्यापक थे इसलिए पिताजी ही हमें पढ़ाते थे।

पिताजी के दो अनुज भी है,पिताजी उनका भी ध्यान रखते थे। हां वह अनुशासन प्रिय हैं,समय पर उठना,समय पर खाना,समय पर सोना उन्हें आज भी पंसद है।

पिताजी कभी भी खाली नहीं बैठते,कुछ न कुछ करते रहते है,जैसे घर व्यवस्थति रखना। वह खाली समय में धामि□क किताबें पढना पसंद करते हैं।

पिताजी कभी भी अपनी जिम्मेदारीयों से मुंह नहीं मोडा,

आज भी हम सब को पूछते रहते हैं, जरूरत पडने पर हर

सम्भव मदद भी करते हैं।

पिताजी से पढ़े छात्र उन्हें आज भी याद करते हैं, उन्हें अपना आदर्श मानते है, पिताजी ने कभी भी किसी से भी बेईमानी नहीं की, कहते है न इमानदारी का कमाया हुआ कभी बेकार नहीं जाता, तभी हम सभी बहने अपने- अपने घरों में खुश हैं।

हम आज भी पिताजी को अपना आदर्श मानते हैं ।

कहते है कि आदमी रिटायर होने के बाद थका थका सा हो जाता है, पर मेरे पिताजी ने रिटायर होने के बाद अपना घर

जो कि आगरा में था को बेचकर हरिद्वार में नया घर लिया।

पिताजी कहते है 'कुछ करना हो तो उम्र आड़े नहीं आती,

हो अगर जजबा कुछ करने का तो ईश्वर स्वंय तुम्हारे पास आता है। '

मुझे याद है वो दिन जब पिताजी हमारे पुराने बैग अपने

विधालय में गरीब बच्चों को दे आते थे, कहते थे उनके पास

किताबें रखने के लिए कुछ नहीं होता।

वह करना चाहते थे उनके लिए बहुत कुछ पर हम छ: बहनों का जिम्मा भी था फिर उस जमाने में एक अध्यापक की इतनी आमदनी नहीं होती थी।

 हम पहले किराये के मकान में रहते थे उसका किराया भी देना होता था।

 पिताजी को खुद रिश्तेदार कहते थे कि क्या करना बेटियों को पढाकर इनकी जल्दी शादी करदो, पर पिताजी ने कभी अहसास नहीं होने दिया हमें पढ़ाया बल्कि छोटी बहन पढ़ाई में काफी अच्छी थी इसलिय उसे दयालबाग से फैशन टैक्सटायल का कोर्स भी कराया।

कहने को बहुत कुछ है पर कुछ धुंधली -धुधंली सी यादे है|

अतः मैं अब समाप्त करती हूँ | आशा करती हूँ कि मेरे पतिाजी के आचरण से ऐसे पतिा को प्रेरणा मलिंगी जो बेटी का जन्म होते ही सर पकड़ लेते है या उसे बोझ समझ मार देते है या बाल वविाह करा देते हैं|

ऊषा भदूला

-0-

Author's Profile

This is Usha Bhadula a homemaker who is very determined and Still hopes to purse her passion of writing. Almost a decade ago she was standing at the crossroad of her life, one road was taking her to pursue teaching and another one was to her family ; She chose her famliy but now here she is following her passion and taking the road not taken.

ushabhadula79@gmail.com

8586964120

<u>Declaration by Author:</u>

This is my original content. I have copyright for this write-up & I am providing project head to use it for publishing with my name.

Usha, Delhi

Usha Shrivastava

देश की शान. भारती सैनकि

जसवंत सिंहि रावत..

ये कहानी है एक ऐसे फौजी की है जसिने अकेले ही चीन के 300 फौजयिों को मारा था 1962 के युद्ध में...

इस बहादुर फौजी का नाम है जसवंत सिंहि रावत. ये उत्तराखंड के रहने वाले थे. इंका जन्म 19 अगस्त 1941 को हुआ था.

ये गड़ वाल राइफ़ल मे भी भर्ती हुए थे. ये बहुत बहादुर सैनकि थे. जब 1962 मे चीन के साथ युद्ध हुआ तब भारत की स्थिति ऐसी थी. की युद्ध से वापस आने का फैसला लेना पढ़ा. लेकनि जसवंत सिंहि रावत ने इस फैसले को नहीं माना. और वापस जाने से मना कर दयिा.

और अकेले ही युद्ध करने लगे.. उन्होंने ऐसी रणनीति बिनाइ की चीन को लगा कि हिज़ारों भारतीय सैनिक युद्ध में है. और एक साथ गोलियां चला रहे हैं.. इस युद्ध में अरुणाचल प्रदेश की दो स्थानीय लड़कियों ने भी जसवंत सिंह का साथ देने आ गई थी. ईन दोनों लड़कियों ने मशीन गन से लगातर गालियां चलाती रहीं. इस तरह चीन के करीब 300 सैनिक अकेले जसवंत सिंह रावत ने मार गिराए. ये युद्ध 72 घण्टे तक चलता रहा. फिर आखिरि कार चीन ने जसवंत सिंह को पकड़ लिया और उनका सर अपने साथ ले गए. जब चीन को पता चला कि इस सैनिक ने अकेले ही युद्ध किया था. चीन के सैनिकों ने पूरे सम्मान के साथ जसवंत सिंह रावत का सर वापस कर दिया. और पूरा सम्मान दिया. और खूब तारीफ की.

आज भी अरुणाचल प्रदेश मे जसवंत सिंह रावत का मंदिर है. सारे फौजी इनको रोज सलाम करते हैं. इनको एक जविति फौजी की तरह मान सम्मान

मलिता है. ये आज भी चीन और भारत के सीमा रेखा की रक्षा करते हैं.

हमारे देश का एक सैनकि चीन के हज़ारों सैनकों को मार सकता है.

सैनकि.. देश की शान

सैनकि देश की शान होता है,

सैनकि देश की आन होता है,

सैनकि देशी की जान होता है,

सैनकों की ताकत से

देश का मान बढ़ता जा रहा है,

देश का तरिगा शान से

पूरे संसार में लहरा रहा है

एक सैनकि कसी का बेटा होता है,

एक सैनकि कसी का पति होता है,

एक सैनकि कसिी का भाई होता है,

ये सारे रश्ते तो बाद मे आते हैं,

सब से पहले एक बहादुर सैनकि देश का होता है,

एक सैनकि देश के लिए सब कुछ कुर्बान कर देता है.

Usha Shrivastava.

-0-

<u>Author's Profile</u>

उषा श्रीवास्तव, कानपुर उत्तर प्रदेश से है. इन्हें लखिना बहुत पसंद है. इनकी कुछ कवतिाएं हनि्दी पात्रकि मे भी छपी है जसिके लिए इन्हें पुरुस्कार भी मलिा है और कई बुक मे सह लेखक भी हुई है. ये सकारात्मक कहानयिा, रोमांटकि कवतिाएं और शायरी लखिती हैं. इनकी कवतिाएं आप instagram @usha2431, sharechat और telegram के चैनल उषा हनि्दी शायरी मे पढ़ सकते हैं

usha.srivastava2020@gmail.com

8957592667

<u>Declaration by Author:</u>

This is my original content. I have copyright for this write-up & I am providing project head to use it for publishing with my name.

Usha Shrivastava, India

शेख़ शहज़ाद उस्मानी

इलाज़ के गहरे राज़

राजा विक्रमादित्य अर्थात 'विक्रम' साहसी, पराक्रमी, समाजसेवी तो थे ही, साथ ही साथ इक्कीसवीं सदी के सामाजिक, राजनीतिक, प्रशासनिक, वैज्ञानिक और मनोवैज्ञानिक ज्ञान से अपडेटिड भी थे यानि ज्ञान के हर क्षेत्र की अद्यतन जानकारी उनको रहती थी। वैज्ञानिक जगत में उन्हें बड़ा सम्मान दिया जाता था, किंतु प्रेमपूर्वक उन्हें 'विक्रम' ही कहा करते थे। वे उनकी बातें मानते थे; यहाँ तक कि उन बातों पर शोध भी करते रहते थे।

दुनिया हर सौ वर्ष में किसी न किसी महामारी के प्रकोप से परेशान हुआ करती थी। इस वर्ष भी एक विषाणु वंश के.नवीन वाइरस ने क़हर बरपा रखा था पूरी दुनिया में। वैज्ञानिकों ने उसे 'नोवेल कोरोना' नाम दे दिया था और उस विषाणु से फैल रही

लाइलाज़ महामारी को 'सार्स-कोवडि-19' नाम दिया गया था। इस महामारी ने दुनिया के सभी देशों में पैर पसार लिए थे क्योंकि यह मानव के मुख और नाक आदि से छूत की बीमारी की तरह संक्रमण फैला रही थी। इस महामारी से बचाव हेतु विश्व कज होनहार वैज्ञानकि सफल वैक्सीन खोजने हेतु रात दनि एक कर रहे थे। वकिसति देशों में होड़ लगी हुई थी पहला वैक्सीन आम जनता तक पहले नंबर पर पहुँचाने हेतु।

इसी सलिसलि में आयोजति एक अंतरराष्ट्रीय वैज्ञानकि सम्मेलन में वक्रिम को भी आमंत्रति किया गया था। वहाँ से लौटने पर वक्रिम ने सोचा कि आयुर्वेद और प्राकृतकि औषधर्यियों का धनी हमारा महान देश भी दुनिया में अव्वल नंबर पर हो सकता है। अपने वृहद ज्ञान के आधार पर उन्होंने एक प्रसद्धि ज्योतषिाचार्य व आयुर्वेद वशिेषज्ञ वैद्य मुनिआदति्यराज से तुरंत सम्पर्क कयिा। उन्होंने महामारी, वाइरस के प्रकारों, उनके

जीवन चक्र और उन पर नियंत्रण के उपाय विषयक
विस्तृत जानकारी दी उनके विनम्र सुझाव के
अनुपालन में विक्रम ने उज्जैन के विशाल जंगल में
योग साधना में लीन योगी दिव्यानन्द से केवल
अकेले जाकर सम्पर्क करने को कहा।

गोपनीय अनुसंधान की महत्वाकांक्षा के साथ
विक्रमादित्य यानि 'विक्रम' रात के घोर अंधकार
में अकेले उज्जैन के घने.जंगलों से होते हुए कई दिनों
जंगली वनस्पतियों और पशु-पक्षियों से जूझते हुए
योगी दिव्यानंद तक पहुँचे। वहाँ का वातावरण
देखकर विक्रम को यह समझने में देर न लगी कि यह
योगी एक बड़ा तांत्रिक भी था। हवन कुण्ड,
नरकंकाल, खोपड़ियाँ और योगी का अद्भुत डरावना
आसन व उसकी काया.... यह सब देख विक्रम को
पहले तो ऐसा लगा कि कि मुनि आदित्यराज से कोई
चूक हुई है और उन्हें ग़लत व्यक्ति के पास भेज
दिया गया है; लेकिन दृढसंकल्पति पराक्रमी

वक्रिम ने प्रणाम कर अपनी समस्या योगी दिव्यानन्द के समक्ष रखी।

पहले तो योगी ने अट्टहास करते हुए कुछ मंत्र उच्चारित किये, फ़िर बोला, "तुम बहादुर हो, ज्ञानी-विशिषज्ञ हो, पराक्रमी-बहादुर हो! इसी लिए तुम्हें मेरे पास भेजा गया है। यहां से पंद्रह किलोमीटर दूर तुम्हें अकेले जाना होगा। एक.विशाल पेड़ पर एक मनुष्य की शव लटका हुआ मिलेगा। वह शव चमगादड़ रूपी बेताल है। उसको पेड़ से उतारकर तुम्हें लाना है। उसे 'नोवेल कोरोना वाइरस' और 'सार्स-कोबडि-19' के लिये ज़िम्मेदार माने जाने वाले चमगादड़ों और मानव जाततिक वाइरस फैलाने वाले तमाम पशु-पक्षियों की गहरी जानकारी तो है ही; वह ही मुझे ही बता सकता है वाइरसों को हराने और महामारियों के बिना साइड इफैक्ट्स वाले शर्तिया इलाज़ के बारे में। वैक्सीन-ऐक्शीन तो बकवास है। हमारे देश में ही महामारियों और वाइरसों का प्राकृतिक अस्त्र-शस्त्र-शास्त्र

है।.... तुम तो बड़े समाजसेवी माने जाते हो न!...
जाओ यथाशीघ्र अपनी पीठ पर ही लादकर उस
बेताल को लेकर आओ अपने देशवासियों की रक्षा
की ख़ातरि!"

विक्रम जो आँखें फाड़-फाड़कर योगी के एक-एक
शब्द कोध्यान से सुन रहा था, योगी दवि्यानन्द के
समक्ष एकदम नतमस्तक हो कर बोला, "जैसी
आज्ञा आपकी योगी जी! ... बताइये... कसि दशिा में
अब मुझे जाना होगा और कसि तरह उस वशिाल
वृक्ष को पहचानना होगा?"

योगी ने इशारे से विक्रम को नज़दीक़ बुलाया और
उसके कान में कहकर सब कुछ गोपनीय समझा दिया।

घने जंगल के बीच चट्टानों, झरनों को पार करता
हुआ विक्रम जंगली वनस्पतियों और खतरनाक पशु-
पक्षयियों से जूझता आख़रि उस स्थान पर पहुंच
गया, जहाँ उस वशिाल वृक्ष पर एक शव उल्टा
लटका हुआ था। यही वह अभीष्ट बेताल था। विक्रम

तुरंत पेड़ पर चढ़ गये। लेकनि अट्टहास करता हुआ बेताल ज़मीन पर गरि गया। वक्रिम ने पेड़ से उतर कर बेताल को क़ाबू में करने की कोशशि की, लेकनि यह क्या... बेताल.पेड़ तक उड़ कर फरि से उल्टा लटक गया। वह लगातार अट्टहास कर वक्रिम का मज़ाक़ उड़ा रहा था। वक्रिम ने दूसरा प्रयास कयिा। कंतिु फ़रि वही हुआ। लेकनि गस बखर.वक्रिम बेताल को कब्ज़े में कर.अपनी पीठ पर लादने में सफल हो गये।

अब वक्रिम यथा शीघ्र बेताल को उस योगी दव्यिानन्द तक पहुँचाने की कोशशि में.जुट गये।

"तो.तुम मुझे उस ढोंगी योगी के सुपुर्द करना चाहते हो वक्रिम!" वक्रिम की पीठ पर.लदा बेताल हँसते हुए बोला।

"जी, अवश्य और शीघ्र ही!" वक्रिम ने उत्तर दयिा।

"रास्ता बहुत लम्बा है! तुम थककर चूर हो जाओगे। बोरियत से उकता जाओगे।.आओ मैं तुम्हें एक कहानी सुनाता हूँ। चुपचाप सुनते रहना। तुम्हारा मुँह खुला और.तुरंत ही उड़कर मैं उस पेड़ पर.वापस लटक जाऊँगा। फिरि तुम मुझे उतार न.सकोगे, समझे न विक्रम!"

"अपने देशवासियों की रक्षा के लिए मुझे तुम्हारी हर शर्त मंजूर है!" विक्रम ने बेताल पर.अपनी पकड़ मज़बूत करते हुए कहा।

"तो सुनो विक्रम! तुम्हारे एक दुश्मन देश की गोपनीय वैज्ञानकि प्रयोगशाला में एक दूसरे विकिसति देश की सेना का शोधार्थी सैनकि-वैज्ञानकि एक चमगादड़ की चीड़-फाड़ कर कोई नया वाइरस खोजने या बनाने की कोशिश कर रहा था!"

विक्रम अपना मुँह बंद रखे हुए बेताल की कहानी सुनने लगे। ......

.....

(मौलकि व स्वरचति)

- शेख़ शहज़ाद उस्मानी

शविपुरी (मध्यप्रदेश)

(रचना तथि- 24-11-2020)

घोषणा - उपरोक्त रचना मेरी मौलकि व स्वरचति रचना है।

शेख़ शहज़ाद उस्मानी

(अशासकीय शक्षिक, लेखक)

बी-2-एस- संतुष्टिअपार्टमेंट्स,

ग्वालयिर बाइपास ए.बी. रोड

उप-डाकघर - कत्था मलि

शविपुरी (मध्यप्रदेश)

पनिकोड - 473-638

कूरियर हेतु शिवपुरी शहर के हेड पोस्ट-ऑफिस का पिनकोड 473551

चलभाष वाट्सएप - 9406589589 (बीएसएनएल)

अन्य - 7987465975 (जियो)

Email :

sheikh.shahzad.usmani.lekhani@gmail.com

-०-

<u>Author's Profile</u>

दमोह (मध्यप्रदेश) में जन्मे वर्तमान में शिवपुरी(मध्यप्रदेश) के स्थायी निवासी शेख़ शहज़ाद उस्मानी एक अशासकीय शिक्षक (पीजीटी), लेखक, आकाशवाणी नैमित्तिक उद्घोषक, रेडियो नाट्यस्वराभिनय कलाकार, यूट्यबर, आर.जे., फेसबुक ब्लॉगर, पोडकास्टर आदि रूप में जाने जाते हैं। आप की मुख्य लेखन विधा लघुकथा विधा है।

आप हाइकु और अन्य शैलियों में काव्य लेखन और गद्य लेखन में भी कलमकार हैं।

आप की लघुकथायें, हाइकु और अन्य रचनायें विभिन्न प्रतिष्ठित पत्र-पत्रिकाओं, साझा संकलनों व स्टोरी मिरर और ओपनबुक्सऑनलाइनडॉटकॉम आदि वेबसाइट्स पर प्रकाशित हो चुके हैं।

आप दिशा प्रकाशन के विश्व हिंदी लघुकथाकार कोश व निदेशिका में भी नामांकित व प्रकाशित किये जा चुके हैं। आप वीडियो लघुकथा/हाइकु/काव्य पाठ भी करते रहते हैं।

 फेसबुक पर आपके द्वारा संचालित लघुकथा पाठ/हाइकु पाठ/काव्य पाठ(जनसंचार; जनमंथन) समूह व पेज हैं और यूट्यब पर चैनल भी (sheikh's language and literature zone) -

शीघ्र ही आपके निजी एकल संग्रहों के प्रकाशन की योजना है।

sheikh.shahzad.usmani.lekhani@gmail.com

9406589589

<u>Declaration by Author:</u>

This is my original content. I have copyright for this write-up & I am providing project head to use it for publishing with my name.

शेख़ शहज़ाद उस्मानी, India

Vashundhra Yadav
Motivational

माना मुश्किल है चलते चले जाना

जब कोई भी साथ न हों।

थोड़ी सी होती हैं बैचेनी

जब हाथो में कोई हाथ न हो

उस बेचैनी को अपनी ताकत बनाना

ताकत के सहारे मंजलि को पाना

मंजलि को पाकर फिर कभी लौट आना

देखना कतिना प्यारा था सफ़र का तराना

–vashundhra(वशु)

-0-

<u>Author's Profile</u>

Poetry princess के नाम से लेखन कार्य करने वाली वशुन्धरा यादव (वशु) मध्य प्रदेश के जिला नरसिंहपुर की रहने वाली हिंदी लिटरेचर की स्नातकोत्तर की छात्रा है इनकी साहित्य में गहरी रुचि और लेखन की कला नित्य लिखने को प्रेरित करती है और ये प्रमुखत प्रेम, ऐतिहासिक, प्रकृतिप्रेम, प्रेरणा दायक आदि प्रकार की रचनाओं को लिखने में रुचि रखती हैं जो instagram,yourquote pe poetry princess या telegram तथा Youtube pe vashus poetry world channel पर उपलब्ध है

vashundhrayadav2000@gmail.com

6267223536

<u>Declaration by Author:</u>

This is my original content. I have copyright for this write-up & I am providing project head to use it for publishing with my name.

Vashundhra yadav, India

डॉ. चंद्रेश कुमार छतलानी / Dr. Chandresh Kumar Chhatlani

At least try

He was running madly. The panic was clearly visible on his face. He was looking back again and again, which caused him to collide with another man. The other man asked, "Hey! Is something wrong?"

He replied in a bewildered voice, "A demon is coming to capture me." The other man looked after him, he too panicked and cried out, "Oho... He's chasing me."

The other man also started running with him. Whoever came across them would see that monster and run with them in panic. The crowd was increasing constantly. Everyone thought that the demon was coming to capture them. Weeks, months and even years passed away. In that crowd, many people got tired and fell, some started crawling. Some of them even stopped with courage, but seeing the terrifying face of the demon and seeing it moving towards them, they started running again.

Eventually a man, who became tired of running and his fear was turning into annoyance, turned and stood up. The demon rushed towards him, seeing that, the man also ran towards the demon with all his might and started fighting with that demon.

And within a few moments he came to know that the demon named Crisis had less power than his energy to escape him.

-0-

प्रयास तो करो

वह बदहवास सा भाग रहा था। उसके चेहरे पर घबराहट स्पष्ट झलक रही थी। वह बार-बार पीछे भी देख रहा था, जिस कारण वह दूसरे आदमी से टकरा गया। उस आदमी ने पूछा, "क्यों भई? क्या हो गया?"

उसने घबराये हुए स्वर में उत्तर दिया, "मेरे पीछे वो राक्षस पड़ा है।" दूसरे आदमी ने उसके पीछे देखा तो वह भी घबरा गया और चिल्ला कर बोला, "अरे! वो तो मेरे पीछे पड़ा है।"

और वह दूसरा आदमी भी उसके साथ भागने लगा। रास्ते में जो भी मिलता, उस राक्षस को देखता और घबराकर उनके साथ भागने लगता। भागने वालों की भीड़ बढ़ती ही जा रही थी। कोई भी नहीं छूट रहा था। सभी को यही प्रतीत हो रहा था कि वह राक्षस उसी के पीछे है। हफ्ते-महीने-साल बीत गए। उस

भीड़ में कितने ही लोग थक कर गिर भी गए, कुछ रेंगने भी लगे थे। उनमें से कुछ लोग साहस करके रुके भी, लेकिन राक्षस का भयानक चेहरा देख और उसे अपनी तरफ बढ़ता पा कर फिर भागने लगे।

आखिरिकार एक आदमी, जो थका नहीं था लेकिन भागने से ऊब गया था और उसका डर खीज में बदलने लगा था, मुड़ कर खड़ा हो गया। राक्षस उसकी तरफ लपका, जिसे देख कर वह आदमी भी अपनी पूरी शक्ति लगाकर राक्षस की तरफ दौड़ा और उस राक्षस से लड़ने लगा।

और कुछ ही क्षणों में उसे पता चल गया कि संकट नाम का वह राक्षस उसकी भागने की ऊर्जा से तो बहुत कम शक्ति रखता था।

-0-

<u>Author's Profile</u>

प्रशिक्षण, शोध, अकादमिक, लेखन, सॉफ़्टवेयर व वेबसाइट निर्माण में 25 से अधिक वर्षों का समृद्ध अनुभव लिए डॉ. चंद्रेश कुमार छतलानी ने 140 से अधिक सॉफ़्टवेयर और वेबसाइट का स्वतंत्र रूप से निर्माण किया गया है। वे दो संस्थाओं ट्रिब्यून इंटरनेशनल वर्ल्डस रिकार्ड्स तथा वर्ल्डस ग्रेटेस्ट रिकॉर्ड से अधिकतम शैक्षणिक प्रमाण पत्र अर्जित करने के रिकॉर्ड धारक भी हैं। इनके अतिरिक्त इनकी अंग्रेजी लघुकथाओं की पुस्तक को भी दो संस्थाओं ने रिकॉर्ड हेतु चयनित किया है।

Dr. Chandresh Chhatlani has over 25 years of experience in Training, Research, Academics, Writing, Software & Website Development. He developed 140+ software & websites. He is a record holder for earning highest academic certificates from two organizations and also a record holder for writing English Laghukathas.

chandresh.chhatlani@gmail.com

9928544749

<u>**Declaration by Author:**</u>

This is my original content. I have copyright for this write-up & I am providing project head to use it for publishing with my name.

-    Dr. Chandresh Kumar Chhatlani, India